50 DAYS OF FAITH

SPIRITUAL GROWTH
STUDY COURSE
Climbing the Faith Ladder

KENNETH SESLEY

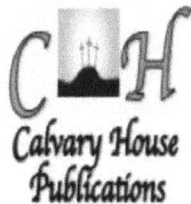

Calvary House
Publications

P. O. Box 781

Lake Elsinore, CA 92531-781

Published by Calvary House Publications
P. O. Box 781, Lake Elsinore, CA
92531-781

C H
Calvary House
Publications

www.RadicalCoaching.com

Ebook edition created in 2013

ISBN 978-1-931820-15-8

Contents:

Introduction:

Through these 50 daily faith lessons, you will be placed in position to systematically maximize your faith by cooperating with God's ordained faith developmental process and thereby maximize your life productivity personally and for the kingdom of God! This course will present, with extreme simplicity, the principles of biblical faith necessary to live a bold, victorious, successful, abundant and overcoming Christian life.

I have been able to determine that there are at least 5 major components of faith that, when implemented, will always produce God's promised results. For the first week, we will introduce you to an understanding of why faith is so important to function successfully in the Kingdom of God. Then for the next five consecutive weeks we will examine one of the major components of the faith regimen each week. During the final week of this spiritual growth campaign, we will bring everything together to insure that you obtain successful results in your faith endeavors.

This course is designed so that for the next 50 Days, you can study and grow in faith working along with a group or independently in this spiritual growth campaign. If you are participating in this spiritual growth campaign with your local church, then you will also want to attend church the next seven Sundays, for the teaching will be on how to develop "great faith". You will also want to attend Sunday School or your small group, for there they will be reinforcing the Sunday morning teachings on faith and going over the answers to the questions at the end of each week's lessons in this book. This course, combined with seven weeks of consistent church attendance and cell group attendance, WILL change your life forever! You may simply read the material each day, or you may get your Bible and read the verses prior to or in addition to reading the devotional material. This is recommended so that you may maximize your faith development. Also, at the bottom of each day's lesson we have a faith confession for you to say. I encourage you to take that confession and repeat it to yourself and God throughout your day.

Enjoy,
Dr. Kenneth R. Sesley

Week No. 1
Understanding the Importance of Faith

Now faith is the substance of things hoped for, the evidence of things not seen. **Hebrews 11:1**

CENTRAL TRUTH: Understanding What Faith is and What Faith is not.

ADDITIONAL VERSES: Luke 18:8; 2 Thessalonians 3:2; James 2:19

In order to properly communicate, one must have a proper understanding of terms. Many people have different ideas about faith. In this course, when we speak of faith, we are talking about the "God kind of faith" or biblical faith. In one sense it is true that every human being has faith. Anytime one sits in a chair without checking to see if it will hold them, or flies on an airplane, they are exercising a natural, ordinary, human faith. However not every human being has the God kind of faith and that is the faith that pleases God.

In the gospel of Luke, Jesus asked the question: "When the Son of man returns, will He find faith on the earth"? If we think of faith in a general sense, then this would be an odd, if not silly question. However we know that the Lord Jesus Christ was not in the business of asking odd or silly questions. Therefore it is apparent that Jesus must have been speaking of a particular type of faith.

Also, in writing to the Thessalonians, the Apostle Paul said: "...all *men* have not faith". Again the Apostle Paul, like the Lord Jesus, couldn't have been speaking about natural human faith. He was speaking about this, "God kind of faith".

The word faith is used in relationship to an institutional commitment to a religious order; for instance, the Baptist Faith, Lutherans, Catholics, Assembly's of God, Charismatic or Word of Faith. However the use of the word "faith" in this course is consistent with the Bible's teachings on this subject. In the Bible, faith is a spiritual action taken to receive or bring to pass a promise of God.

The simplest way to define Bible faith is, "Faith is ***believing*** and ***acting*** like the Word of God is true". Therefore we see that biblical faith requires at least two components: belief and action. Faith is not true Bible faith when it is only belief. It's belief. The Bible says that demons believe and tremble, but they don't act in line with the Word of God. In fact they act totally opposite of the Word of God. Also, faith is not true Bible faith when it is only acting. Acting without believing is simply foolishness, and it will not produce biblical results.

FAITH CONFESSION:

Because God told me to have faith in Him, I have the ability to use my faith!

WEEK 1
Understanding the Importance of Faith:
Day 2
The Importance of Faith to Every Believer

"For whatever is born of God overcomes the world: and this is the victory that has overcome the world, even our faith" **(1 John 5:4).**

CENTRAL TRUTH: The Critical Nature of the Development of Faith in the life of the believer.

ADDITIONAL VERSES: Habakkuk 2:4; Romans 10:10; Romans 10:17; Hebrews 10:38; 2 Corinthians 5:7; Mark 9:23; Hebrews 11:5; Galatians 3:13-14; Matthew 9:22; Matthew 9:29; Matthew 13:58; Mark 6:5-6; Romans 4:16

Once you accept Jesus Christ as your Savior and Lord, you are as saved as you will ever be. However, if you are going to live a bold, victorious, overcoming, healthy and abundant Christian life; your salvation experience must be followed up by spiritual growth and development. This is called discipleship. At the church I pastor, Calvary Fellowship International, we exist to Make Disciples that Multiply, Dominate and Make a Difference in their world and around the world. Faith is the foundation from which all discipleship can occur. In the book of Hebrews, the Bible declares that without faith, it is impossible to please God. The Apostle Peter told us that we are to "add to our faith". Therefore, as I said, faith is the foundation from which all discipleship occurs.

Remember that the simplest definition of faith is: "...acting and believing that God's Word is true". Through faith we believers may tap into the supernatural power of God made available to Christians, so that we can transform our circumstances, conditions and situations in life, based on the will of God as revealed in the Scriptures.

The Prophet Habakkuk told us that the just (those who have been declared righteous by believing in and receiving the Lord Jesus Christ as Savior and Lord) are to live their lives out through faith. The Apostle Paul quoted from this passage several times and went on to inform us that we as believers are to walk by faith and not by sight. To walk by faith means to conduct our daily lives by faith.

In fact the writer of Hebrews expressed the importance of faith by telling us that without faith, it is absolutely impossible to please God. I know of no other subject or theme in the Scriptures that the Bible tells us that without this, it is impossible to please God. As important as love is, the Bible doesn't tell us that without it, it is impossible to please God. Of course the Bible says that faith works by love, but what this verse actually means is that our faith works according to our understanding of God's love for us. Though it has been preached as if it refers to the way we walk in love, the context of this passage doesn't mean that. Faith in God actually rests on our revelation of God's love for us. Faith works by that love. Now don't misunderstand me; it is essential that we walk in love. Love is the no. 1 and no. 2 commandments of the Bible. Love God with all of your heart, et. al., and love your neighbor as yourself. That sums up all of God's commands.   Still there is nowhere in the Bible that God came right out and said, "Without love it is impossible to please Me". So you can see that it is critical that you and I master the principles of biblical faith, so that we can please God!

From our foundational verse in 1 John, we find that faith is necessary to overcome the challenges of life. Jesus taught His disciples that their association with Him would not exempt them from experiencing the challenges of life. Our covenant with God is not a panacea against negative circumstances and challenges. Our covenant is a commitment from God that when we exercise our faith in the promises of Scriptures, we can overcome any and all problems that life & the kingdom of darkness may bring our way!

We also find in the book of Galatians that *faith is the key to receiving the promises of God*. In Chapter 3, verses 13 and 14, the Apostle Paul told us that Christ has redeemed us from the curse of the law, by hanging on the cross of Calvary. As Jesus hung on that cross, He took the punishment for all of our sins by being our substitute. By so doing, He also entitled us to receive the blessing of Abraham. Abraham's blessing was primarily three-fold: 1. A Financial or Material Blessing, 2. A Physical Blessing of health and longevity of life and 3. A Spiritual Blessing, which involved a future relationship with God through Christ for Abraham and his descendants. Receiving Jesus Christ has brought us into position to receive this three-fold blessing! However Paul tells us that this blessing is received "through <u>faith</u>".

Even during the earthly ministry of Jesus, as He would minister healing to people, He would tell them that their capacity to receive was on the basis of their faith. In fact the Bible tells us that on one occasion Jesus actually failed to bring to pass the results that He desired in the lives of the people of Nazareth. Actually it wasn't a failure on Jesus' part...the failure was on the people's behalf relative to them not exercising faith. The Bible says that Jesus *could* do no mighty works in Nazareth because of the people's unbelief or lack of faith! It didn't say that He <u>would</u> do no mighty works there because of their unbelief. It says HE COULD DO NO MIGHTY WORKS BECAUSE OF THEIR UNBELIEF. So unbelief stops the power of God from flowing into the human situation.

This should settle the questions that many believers have about why some believers experience the good things of life that God has promised to us and why others don't. This is why believers live at various levels of blessings in their lives. It is not that God is withholding anything from them. It is not that God is being a respecter of persons. It's just that God has designed the system in such a way that in order to receive from Him, it must be done on the basis of faith. God did this so that every believer could receive from Him strictly on the basis of God's grace and not human merits!

For years I've watched as some believers continue to grow and expand their capacity to believe and receive from God, while others have stayed at the same level of receiving. They do receive on a low level, but God has promised them so much more. God wants each of His children doing good works and involved in projects that bless the world. The goal of this 50-DAYS OF FAITH Spiritual Growth Study Course is to cause you to rise to a level of faith that allows you to complete faith projects that have the potential to bless the world!

FAITH CONFESSION:
My faith in God gives me the victory over every circumstance in life!

Week 1
Understanding the Importance of Faith:
Day 3
Do Not Confuse the Three Biblical types of Faith

"For I say, through the grace given to me, to everyone who is among you, not to think of himself more highly than he ought to think, but to think, soberly, as God has dealt to each one a measure of faith". (**Romans 12:3**)

CENTRAL TRUTH: Though faith is the same in essence and operation, sometimes faith functions differently.

ADDITIONAL VERSES: Ephesians 2:8; Romans 10:17; 1 Corinthians 12:7-9, 11; Mark 11:22-24

As we study the Scriptures, we discover that there are several types of faith mentioned in the Bible. Also, there are also several "degrees" or levels of faith. Today we will examine the three types of faith that are prominently mentioned in the Scriptures.

First, there is what is called, "God's saving" faith. This type of faith is spoken of in the book of Ephesians. It is the simple faith that comes into our heart when we hear the gospel message of salvation preached or shared with us and the Holy Spirit brings conviction to our hearts or opens our eyes to the truth about our need for Jesus. This is the measure of faith spoken of in Romans 12:3.

Then there is the Gift of Faith as mentioned in the 12th Chapter of 1 Corinthians. The Apostle Paul there tells us that there is a special manifestation that the Holy Spirit imparts to believers on special occasions, as He wills (vs.11), in order to accomplish the will of God through the supernatural intervention or infusion of faith. An example of this kind of faith can be seen in the life of the prophet Daniel when he was thrown into the lions' den. Naturally anyone would be terrified if they were thrown into a den of hungry lions. However through the gift of faith or special faith, as the Amplified Version calls it, Daniel was able to trust God in this extraordinary circumstance, and miraculously, the lions didn't eat him. It is not our objective in this study course to go into any more detail about this type of faith.

Finally, there is the "God Kind of Faith". Understanding thoroughly this kind of faith is what these 50 Days of Faith is all about! In Mark 11:22, Jesus said: "Have faith in God..." However, if you could read this from the original Greek language, it would read, "Have the faith of God". Well if you had the faith of God, then you would have the "God Kind of Faith". So what our Lord was telling us is that God has given His followers the ability to exercise faith along the same lines as God Himself does. Therefore things that we find in Scriptures regarding God's faith are indicators of how believers can and should utilize their own faith. Thus it is not wrong to imitate God's utilization of His faith, because Jesus Himself told us to have the God kind of faith!

FAITH CONFESSION:

I have the God kind of faith that can change my world!

WEEK 1
Understanding the Importance of Faith:
Day 4
There are Several Levels or Degrees of Faith

"For I say, through the grace given to me, to everyone who is among you, not to think of himself more highly than he ought to think, but to think, soberly, as God has dealt to each one a measure of faith". (**Romans 12:3**)

CENTRAL TRUTH: You and I must take our measure of faith and develop it.

ADDITIONAL VERSES: Mark 4:35-41; Mt. 6:30; Luke 12:28; Matt. 8:23-26; 14:22-31; 16:1-10; Romans 4:19; Romans 4:17-20; 2 Thessalonians 1:3.

Several years ago, my wife and I attended a Kenneth E. Hagin Campmeeting in Tulsa, OK. During the morning session Dr. Fred Price, pastor of Crenshaw Christian Center, was the daily teacher. He taught a message that addressed the fact that there are various levels of faith and that it was and is possible for a person's faith to be highly developed in one area, and not in another area. This teaching made it so very clear why one person could be highly developed in faith so that they could receive healing, but yet constantly struggle in the area of receiving God's financial blessings. Again, as Romans 12:3 reveals, we all began with the same measure of faith. Dr. Price explained that faith is like a muscle. A perfectly healthy baby has been given the same amount of muscles as a full grown adult. However, as you know, that baby has to grow and develop their muscles through proper diet and exercise. Dr. Price went on to tell us that it is the same with faith. I never forgot that teaching and I have made it my life long pursuit to continue to develop my faith and to help others develop their faith.

Now in order for you to develop your faith, you must recognize that the Lord Jesus and His Apostles recognized that there are various levels or degrees of faith, which the Bible mentions:

First the Lord Jesus spoke of "no" faith in the gospel of Mark. So again it is possible to not have any of the God kind of faith at all.

Second, Jesus spoke of "little" faith as recorded in five places in the gospels. This is faith that is too weak to believe God's Word to bring to pass God's promised results in one's own life.

The Apostle Paul also spoke of "weak" faith in the book of Romans. Weak faith looks at or considers or contemplates fully the negative circumstances confronting it then it forms an opinion of things that is contrary to the promise of God through unbelief.

In that same chapter, the Apostle Paul also mentions "strong" faith. Strong faith confidently expects to receive something good when there are no natural reasons for it to, based only on the promise of God. In the book of 2nd Thessalonians the Bible teaches us that our faith can and should grow!

FAITH CONFESSION:

I will feed my faith daily so that it can grow exceedingly into strong faith!

Bless the Lord, O my soul, and forget not all of His benefits **(Psalm 103:2).**

CENTRAL TRUTH: Faith unlocks the powerful benefits of being a believer in Christ!

ADDITIONAL VERSES: Luke 17:5; 1 John 5:4; Hebrews 6:12; 2 Corinthians 13:11; Isaiah 28:10; 1 Corinthians 10:11; Matthew 9:23; Habakkuk 2:4; 2 Peter 1:2-4; John 10:10; Hebrews 6:12

We have already seen that through faith we believers may tap into the supernatural power of God made available to Christians, so that we can transform our circumstances, conditions and situations in life, based on the will of God as revealed in the Scriptures. When we study faith in the life and teachings of Jesus, we find that there was always a positive tangible benefit from operating in biblical faith. It is apparent that Jesus' apostles also saw something beneficial to operating in faith, because they asked Jesus to increase their faith. Today, we will look at several of these benefits as revealed in Scriptures.

As we have already seen, faith is the key to overcoming the negative circumstances and situations that come to us in life. In the book of Hebrews, we find that God can use our example of faith as an inspiration to others in their faith walk. Then in Matthew 9, we find that we can have our possibilities in life become limitless, by operating in faith. In the book of Habakkuk and in the book of Romans, we discover that by living by faith, we can experience the highest quality of life there is. Both the Hebrew word used in Habakkuk and the Greek word used in Romans refer to the highest kind of life. The Greek word for life is Zoë, which means, life at its extreme or the God kind of life. You see it takes the God kind of faith to live the God kind of life!

In 2 Peter the Apostle Peter tells us that God, through His divine power, has given to us all things that pertain to life and godliness. This means not just all things for living a godly or spiritual life, but all things for living naturally here on the earth. Jesus said that He came that we might have life and that more abundantly. In 2 Peter, he also told us that God has given to you and me exceedingly great and precious promises and that through these promises you and I can partake of the "divine nature" of God and escape the corruption that is in the world! The Apostle Paul lets us know, in the 6th chapter of the Book of Hebrews, that we inherit or obtain these promises through faith and patience.

FAITH CONFESSION:

I am able to obtain God's promises from Him with my faith!

WEEK 1
Understanding the Importance of Faith:
Day 6
Make the Decision to Increase Your Faith

[5]And the apostles said to the Lord "Increase our faith." [6]So the Lord said, "If you have faith as a mustard seed, you can say to this mulberry tree, 'Be pulled up by the roots and be planted in the sea,' and it would obey you. **Luke 17:5-6 (NKJV)**

ADDITIONAL VERSES: Hebrews 12:1-2; 2 Timothy 2:15; Joshua 1:8; 1 Corinthians 15:10; Romans 5:2

CENTRAL TRUTH: Increasing your faith is not up to the Lord...it's up to you.

Whenever one makes a quality decision, it causes several other decisions to be made for them almost automatically. For example, I made a decision to follow Christ the summer of 1978. With that decision was the decision to live a godly lifestyle because I did not want to live as a hypocrite. So likewise as you make the decision to develop your faith, other decisions are inherent in this quality decision.

Now before you can make a quality decision, you must know what a quality decision is. A quality decision is a decision from which there is no turning back from regardless of the contrary circumstances that will confront you in an attempt to cause you to change your mind. In week six we will show how and what it takes to make a strong commitment that cannot be shaken, once you have made a quality decision.

Making a quality decision to increase your faith requires that you must make three other choices:

First you must anticipate resistance from Satan, society and even the saints.

o   We have an archenemy named Satan or the devil. There is only one Satan or devil, but there are many demons. Satan and his cadre of demons will do everything within their power to distract you or discourage you from developing your faith; but you must learn to walk in perseverance and persistence and see your decision through to the end.

o   In addition to our archenemy Satan, society will try to hinder you from sticking with your decision. Society refers to people outside of the church. Unchurched people have an entirely different set of values from that of the Word of God, and they will try to get you to continue life as you lived it before you were born again.

o   But there is another group, called the saints, who also will sometimes hinder you from your commitment to increase your faith. This doesn't refer to all Christians; just most of them. It's sad, but it's true, that most Christians never make a commitment to develop their faith; and some of them will even try to hinder you in your efforts to develop your faith. They will say, "Child it doesn't take all that. Just be like me and go to church on Sundays...when you can...and you will be a good Christian like me". These are the same people, who are sick, critical, angry, bitter, broke, busted and/or disgusted, and can't understand why they are. They blame everything either on God, the devil or other people. Everyone but the right person; themselves. You don't want to be like them at all. They are self-deceived, which is the worst deception there is.

Second, you must determine to become a serious student of the Word of God (the Bible).

o The Bible tells us that we must study to show ourselves approved of God as a person that needs not to be ashamed. It tells us that we must meditate in God's Word day and night, so that we can observe to do it, and then we will prosper and have good success.

Third, you must adopt a lifestyle that is designed to make you become all that you can be for Christ.

o The Bible tells us that it is by grace that we become all that God wants us to be and we only have the capacity to walk in that grace by walking by faith.

o This third decision means that you have made an automatic choice to rise above an average, mediocre lifestyle into the lifestyle of an uncommon believer who is an uncommon achiever!

In our foundational passage for this lesson the apostles asked Jesus to increase their faith. However He, in so many words, told them to do something with the measure of faith that they had. He put it like this: If you have faith like a grain of mustard seed, then begin to speak what you believe and your faith will grow and work. In other words faith is like a seed. Plant it and it will grow. When it grows, it will move contrary circumstances and challenges in your life. I want to encourage you and even challenge you to make a quality decision to increase your faith level by operating in the Scriptural principles that will enable you to do so, and then developing a strong commitment to maintain your course till you arrive at your victory in every faith endeavor!

FAITH CONFESSION:

I am able to obtain the promises of God with my faith!

²²So Jesus answered and said to them, "Have faith in God. ²³For assuredly, I say to you, whoever says to this mountain, 'Be removed and be cast into the sea,' and does not doubt in his heart, but believes that those things he says will be done, he will have whatever he says. **Mark 11:22-23 (NKJV)**

CENTRAL TRUTH: Your faith needs a proper Biblical foundation to build upon.

ADDITIONAL VERSES: 2 Timothy 2:15; 2 Peter 1:20; Isaiah 28:11-13; Mark 11:22-24

Operating in faith has been grossly misunderstood. Some have attempted to operate in "faith" without a scriptural foundation for their actions. Remember earlier we said that faith can be defined as ***believing*** and ***acting*** like the Word of God is so. We also stated that believing without acting is just belief or we could say "mental assent" or "mental agreement". However acting without believing is foolishness and even being presumptuous.

Many inappropriate actions and mistakes have been blamed on walking by faith. This study course is founded upon what the Word of God says about the subject of faith. That's the only true foundation for faith. In the midst of critics teaching against operating in the God-kind of faith, it is imperative that the Word of God be rightly divided or accurately interpreted, so that there will be no mistakes made in regards to what the Bible teaches about this most important subject.

First of all, the Bible teaches that there is no private interpretation of Scriptures, which implies that there must be rules for proper interpretation of the Scriptures. The rules for interpreting the Bible are simple and recognized by all Bible Scholars of every denomination (though they aren't always followed due to religious biases, unbelief and pre-conceived ideas about what the Bible says). Below you will find these rules, which must be respected for consistency and accuracy in extracting truths from the Word of God by which you and I are to live by:

First, Scriptures must be interpreted with contextual consistency. If the context is talking about something natural, then we can't "spiritualize" its meaning and ignore what is being talked about.

Second, any truth critical for the believer to live by must be seen in both precept and example. Precept is the principle underlined explained and example is the principle portrayed in the life of God's people. If you can't find both the precept and the example in Scripture, don't build a doctrine or belief around some isolated passage of Scripture.

Finally, any principle important to the believer's life should be seen in at least two or three scriptural references. One should also look for at least two or three examples found in the scriptures as well.

Bishop Ira Hilliard said: "For every promise of scriptures, every principle found in God's Word and every prophecy that comes from the Spirit of God, there is a faith process to bring it to pass". So you and I must understand that faith is not an event; it is a process. Learning the process is crucial for the effective operation of faith. Mark 11:22-24 reveals the faith process, as directly spoken from the lips of the Lord Jesus. Next week we will examine these verses (especially vs. 23) in order to gain a thorough understanding of the faith process.

ASSIGNMENTS

1. Familiarize yourself with the faith scriptures from this week's lessons.

2. Complete the study questions from week one.

3. Attend Church on Sunday services and a Growth Group next week.

FAITH CONFESSION:

Through Faith I can remove every mountain in my life.

1. What is the definition of faith as stated in this Study Course?

2. List five reasons why faith is so important to the believer?

   _____

   _____

   _____

   _____

   _____

3. List the three types of biblical faith mentioned in this section.

   _____

   _____

   _____

4. List the three aspects of consistent and accurate scriptural interpretation?

   _____

   _____

   _____

Week No. 2
The Faith Regimen - Component 1: Asking

WEEK 2
The Regimen of Faith – Component 1: <u>A</u>sking
Day 8
The Importance of Receiving Instruction in Faith

⁵And the Apostles said to the Lord, "Increase our faith." ⁶So the Lord said, "If you have faith as a mustard seed, you can say to this mulberry tree, 'Be pulled up by the roots and be planted in the sea,' and it would obey you. **Luke 17:5-6 (NKJV)**

CENTRAL TRUTH: Instruction in Faith is Critical for the Development of Your Faith.

ADDITIONAL VERSES: Mark 4:3, 14; Romans 10:17; Romans 4:17; 2 Corinthians 5:7; 1 Corinthians 14:40; 2 Timothy 3:16-17; Proverbs 20:5

I want to remind you of our working definition of faith, which is this: Faith is believing and acting like the Word of God is true. We also see that faith is a spiritual principle that allows believers to tap into the supernatural power of God made available to Christians, so that we can transform our circumstances, conditions and situations in life, based on the will of God as revealed in the Scriptures. For every promise of Scripture, for every principle of biblical success and for every prophecy born of the Spirit of God, there is a faith process or regimen to bring it to pass. This begins the first of five weeks of us examining the five major components of the faith regimen. Today we begin with component one, the "asking" component of the faith process. But before we do this, I want to discuss the critical nature of being instructed in faith and things that you should expect through the faith process.

In our golden text above, we see that the Apostles needed instruction in faith because of their lack of understanding of the way that faith comes and the way faith works. They thought that faith was something that Jesus could increase in them apart from any actions done by them. However Jesus taught them differently. He explained that faith begins as a seed. According to **Mark 4:3 & 14,** the seed of faith is contained in the Word of God. Faith ***comes*** by hearing and hearing by the Word of God. But, according to our passage in Luke, faith ***grows*** by continually saying what you desire to come to pass, as if it has already come to pass. You must hear the Word of God until the truth dawns on your heart. You see as a minister shares the Word of God, he gives you <u>information</u>. But until the Word of God comes alive inside of you, it's still not <u>revelation</u>. As you then study, mediate upon, confess and act upon God's Word, then you will see <u>transformation</u>.

The Word of God is our textbook for faith that gives us the foundation in faith. Paul told his disciple, and co-worker in ministry, Timothy (who was pastoring at the time) that the Word of God provides us four things:

1. DOCTRINE – Teaching or **information** about the established order of God. The Word of God will give us the information we need about the established order of God
2. REPROOF – The **conviction** that challenges erroneous thinking. The Word of God will convict us so that we have the capacity to eliminate erroneous thinking from our lives if we will allow it to.
3. CORRECTION – This is the **formation** (or rectification) of God's truth in our minds in such a way

that causes us to straighten up in our daily lifestyle. The Word of God will enable us to assimilate the truth of God into our thinking, bringing us correction.

4. INSTRUCTION – This is the full **education** that brings the knowledge, skill, and understanding that is required so that we can use our faith in a systematic way so that [we] may be complete, thoroughly equipped for every good work.

When we go to the Word of God to get our foundation in faith it will (1) give us the established order of God and it will (2) eliminate erroneous thinking. This is necessary because before we were exposed to truth, every one of us were exposed to error (and out right lies) which resulted in erroneous thinking. The Word of God will also (3) cause the formation of God's truth into our thinking and (4) we will become knowledgeable, skillful and able to use our faith in a systematic way so that we may be complete, thoroughly equipped to do God's work. You must recognize that God is a God of order, and therefore He has an orderly or systematic way of approaching Him with the God kind of faith. We will then arrive at a state of maturity where operating and walking by faith will be a part of our very nature!

When one begins to understand the Word of God and begins walking by faith they must understand that there are several things that will precede the actual manifestation that their faith is working to bring to pass. There are six things that you can expect to come to pass as you walk through the faith process:

1. Wisdom, which is an accurate application of knowledge, both naturally and spiritually, at every stage of the faith process.

2. Favor, which is the divinely inspired desire of others to assist you in what you are believing for, by using their wisdom, ability, influence, power, and even their finances.

3. A Plan of Action, which is a divinely inspired series of steps necessary to bring the acquisition of what you desire.

4. Sustenance, which is God's provision until your manifestation occurs (**2 Cor. 9:8-10**)

5. Strength to endure through the spiritual wherewithal that God gives so one may patiently hold their course until they see the manifestation!

6. A Miracle, which is the supernatural intervention of God suspending natural laws

FAITH CONFESSION:

I have a teachable attitude so that I can maximize my faith.

WEEK 2
The Regimen of Faith – Component 1: <u>A</u>sking
Day 9
Respecting the Order of God is Fundamental to the Development of Faith

Let all things be done decently and in order **(1 Corinthians 14:40).**

CENTRAL TRUTH: Our faith must operate according to God's order, not our opinion.

ADDITIONAL VERSES: Hebrews 11:3; Mark 4:26-28; Mark 11:23-25; James 2:14

Unfortunately, most believers have little respect for the order of God (doctrine) because their thinking has been dominated by tradition. As previously stated, God is a God of order and He works a certain way. This statement does not take anything away from the sovereignty of God, nor does it dishonor Him. God in His sovereignty has chosen to conduct Himself in an orderly manner or systematic way. First, this is because it is the wisest course of action or the universe would be in total chaos. Second, God has a passion to be believed and trusted. There would be no way that anyone could trust Him if He didn't operate in an orderly manner.

You must understand that it is the consistent nature of God to function with order. Natural order is easily seen in the natural elements and we can see God's order in those elements. The reason we are able to send a person out into space and bring them safely back is because there is a consistent order in the way things operate in the natural. The reason a doctor can operate on a person, open them up, take out their heart and replace it again is because there is consistent order in the human body. We have to appreciate the structure of things in the natural. We have to believe that when it comes to God's prized possession, His relationship with man, He would also deal with us according to order.

We can see spiritual order in the Word of God. In the Scriptures, we are commanded to do things decently and in order. If He tells us to deal with things according to order, He Himself is our model. **<u>Faith is a process and the results are progressive.</u>** If you can respect the order of things and respect the progressive manifestations of receiving the things that you are believing for, you will not get frustrated. **You don't have to know how it is going to work out.** You just need to understand the process and how to make it work in your life.

The Bible describes the Word working process or the faith process as getting results progressively. As you begin to work the process, you may get small results at first. The *principle* of the God kind of faith is found in Mark 11:23. The *principle* of the God kind of faith is this: you will have what you say with your mouth and believe in your heart...good or bad. Then in vs. 24, we find the *prayer* of faith. The prayer of faith is this: you will have what you believe you receive when you pray. We can see three major components of faith associated with the prayer of faith: Asking, Believing and Confessing. I call this the A, B, C's of faith.

Just as in any other situation, to maximize the system we must learn the laws of the system. You don't have to know the laws of this land to live in this land, but in order to live with the benefits of your rights; you need to know the laws. When you know the laws you can keep people from encroaching upon your rights. Therefore it is important to understand the order of God to live an exceptional lifestyle in the Kingdom of God.

The profile of an example of the faith process can be found in Romans 4:17-20. As we can see Abraham working the principle, we are able to reference each component back to him–the father of faith. His situation had more impossibility attached to it than anything that you are going through. He was promised at an old age that he would have a son and that he would be the father of many nations. He waited for this promise for twenty-five years. The natural that it takes to produce a child was not working within him at the age of one hundred and his wife's womb was dead. Everything in the natural that would make the promise come to pass for Abraham was not working. God taught him systematically how to walk in faith and how to exercise his faith so that God could get the promise to him. Although God wanted it to happen for Abraham, He could not bless Abraham until He could respond to Abraham's faith for it.

There are some things that God really wants for you but He can't give them to you until you can receive them by faith. If Abraham waited twenty-five years with discipline, you can wait a few days or months. This is a faith process, not magic. This is not a get rich quick scheme. It is a disciplined lifestyle where you tap into the supernatural power of God that is made available to you to change natural circumstances, situations, and conditions over which you have been given authority. When you understand God's order, you gain confidence. Then all you have to do is work on your faith.

FAITH CONFESSION:

I can have what I say with my mouth from a believing heart.

Ask, and it shall be given you... **(Matthew 7:7a)**

CENTRAL TRUTH: It is the will of God that you and I ask Him for the things we need, want and desire.

ADDITIONAL VERSES: Hebrews 4:16; 2 Peter 1:3-4; 1 Chronicles 4:10;

In today's lesson we will discover that, not only should we not be embarrassed to ask God for things but, we should be bold in our requests to God. The Word of God clearly teaches that we should ask God for everything that we need, want and desire, that is consistent with a godly lifestyle. There is no need for you to feel uneasy or apologetic about asking. It is important to the successful operation of your faith that you understand that God Himself has declared that He wants you to ask Him for any and everything that you want, need, and desire that is consistent with a Godly lifestyle found in the Word of God.

The Word of God is our final authority. So, rather than you having to take my word on the matter, or any other person that you believe is a credible authority, we will go directly to the Scriptures and use them as our basis for believing. Several years ago there was a popular book out called the Prayer of Jabez. In it we are told that Jabez asked God and God granted him his desire. I want to give you several verses that show us that asking is the will of God for you and me.

23"And in that day you will ask Me nothing. Most assuredly, I say to you, whatever you ask the Father in My name He will give you. 24Until now you have asked nothing in My name. Ask, and you will receive, that your joy may be full. **John 16:23-24 (NKJV)**

If you abide in Me, and My words abide in you, you will ask what you desire, and it shall be done for you. **John 15:7 (NKJV)**

14Now this is the confidence that we have in Him, that if we ask anything according to His will, He hears us. 15And if we know that He hears us, whatever we ask, we know that we have the petitions that we have asked of Him. **1 John 5:14-15 (NKJV)**

In our last passage, we see the word petition. The Bible mentions various types of prayer, such as the prayer of intercession, the prayer of consecration, the prayer of thanksgiving and the prayer of praise, just to mention a few. My mentor, the late Dr. Kenneth E. Hagin, used to say that the problem with the church is that we have taken all prayer and put them in a bag together, shaken it up and thrown them out and expected them to work. However just as baseball, basketball, football and hockey are all sports, each of these sports has different rules that govern them. Prayer is the same way. Each of these various types of prayer has different rules. In this study guide, we are only addressing what has been deemed, the prayer of faith, or the prayer of petition. In the next lesson we will give you seven (7) rules involved in asking.

Remember this though regarding the Prayer of Faith:

In Mark 11:24, the Lord said: Whatever **_you_** desire, when **_you_** pray, believe that **_you_** receive them and **_you_** will have them. The prayer of faith is primarily a prayer for you! All of the concepts or principles contained in this book address praying for one's own personal needs, wants and desires, and not for the needs of others. Because faith is the same in essence and faith is involved in each type of praying, some of these principles will be the same. My objective in this book is to teach you how to get your own personal answers to prayer and not to teach you how to pray for others right now. That will have to come in another book.

FAITH CONFESSION:

My Father God gets joy when I ask for what I need.

WEEK 2
The Regimen of Faith — Component 1: <u>A</u>sking
Day 11
How to Ask God's Way (Part 1)

And in that day you shall ask me nothing. Most assuredly I say to you, whatever you ask the Father in My name he will give you. **(John 16:23).**

CENTRAL TRUTH: You need to understand the rules that govern prayer.

ADDITIONAL VERSES: Mark 11:24; John 16:23; 1 Timothy 6:17; 1 John 5:14 Romans 8:17; Gal. 3:29; 4:7; Heb. 1:4

Rule No. 1: You Must Have an "Eligible Desire". Through the Bible, God has let us know His general will for what He wants us to have. We cannot ask God for another man's husband or another man's wife, because that would be both covetousness and adultery. Anything that would put you into a sinful position will make your petition an "out of bounds" request. However, we can ask God for anything for our enjoyment that is consistent with a godly lifestyle, because God wants our joy to be full.

We can ask God for anything that we find in the written Word of God, which we call the Logos. There is peace in the Word of God, therefore you can ask for peace. There is freedom from worry in the Word of God, therefore you can ask for a worry free lifestyle without being ashamed.

We can also use our faith to petition God for anything that the Spirit of God reveals to us that He wants us to have or do. This will always be consistent with the principles contained in the written Word of God. You may not be able to find in the Word of God that God wants you to drive a nice car, but it does say, "Be it unto you according to your faith". If you need a nice car to go to work so you will have seed to sow and money to take care of your household (which are God's revealed will) then you can believe for it. Having a nice car does not violate any godly principle in the Word.

Rule No 2: You Must Ask God the Father in the name of Jesus. According to John 16:23, we don't ask Jesus for anything when we pray. We do not ask for Jesus' sake. Jesus doesn't need the car, you do. To ask in Jesus' name means to ask, based on His authorization for us to ask from His account. We are heirs to the use of His name.

Rule No 3: You Must Ask according to God's Will. It is critical that you be instructed in the Word of God so that you will know what the Will of God is. God's Will is found in His Word. If you ask according to His Will, then you will have a strong confidence that He has heard you. This confidence doesn't come by how you feel, but by what His Word says. God has never asked us to judge the effectiveness of our prayers by what we feel.

FAITH CONFESSION:

My Father God gets joy when I ask for [and receive] what I need.

WEEK 2
The Regimen of Faith – Component 1: <u>A</u>sking
Day 12
How to Ask God's Way (Part 2)

And in that day you shall ask me nothing. Most assuredly I say to you, whatever you ask the Father in My name he will give you. **(John 16:23).**

CENTRAL TRUTH: You need to understand the rules that govern prayer.

ADDITIONAL VERSES: James 1:6-7; Hebrews 11:1; 1 John 5:14-15; Philippians 4:6-7

Rule No. 4: You <u>Must</u> Ask Without Wavering. The Apostle James said that if you waver (or doubt), you will not receive anything from God. Therefore, once you have found the will of God from the Word of God or the Spirit of God, you must ask one time with thanksgiving and without wavering. By repeating this request for your personal petition, you are in unbelief. If you believe that God heard you when you prayed, and you believed that you received it when you prayed, then you have it. When you ask, you receive it spiritually before it ever becomes yours in the natural. You have to work the rest of the faith process to bring it to pass.

Rule No. 5: You <u>Must</u> *Be Specific* in Your Asking. Without a clear blueprint, your faith has nothing to give substance to. You must make your request so specific that you can easily and quickly recognize any counterfeit that the devil tries to send to you. You must become pregnant with what you desire in your imagination, clearly seeing it as yours. Don't compromise on exactly what you are believing for. We will show you the importance of this and how this is done next week.

Rule No. 6: You <u>Must</u> *Verbalize Your Prayer* so that it can be heard. Nowhere in the Bible does it tell us to pray a silent prayer. The Bible tells us that we must open up our mouths and tell God exactly what we want in prayer. Notice what it says: If we <u>ASK</u> according to His will, He "HEARS" us. "This means that we are verbalizing our request or petition as we pray. We can only know that he HEARS us if we ASK aloud. Some people counter by saying, "Well God knows my heart". This is true. In Matthew 6, the Bible says that God knows not only your heart but He also knows your needs before you ever pray; but Jesus still tells us that we must ask aloud. If He didn't mean aloud or there was no need to ask aloud, then God would just read our heart or mind and examine our needs and give us what we need or what He wants us to have. But that is contrary to what the Bible teaches. Just as a parent wants their child to come to them and ask, rather than to drop hints, so does God our Heavenly Father.

Rule No. 7: You <u>Must</u> Add Continual Thanksgiving to Your Asking. Once you have prayed in faith, you are to then continue to thank God for it until you see it manifested in your life.

FAITH CONFESSION:
Whatever qualified desire I ask for, in Jesus name, I will receive.

For my thoughts are not your thoughts, neither are your ways my ways, saith the LORD. For as the heavens are higher than the earth, so are my ways higher than your ways and my thoughts than your thoughts. **(Isaiah 55:8-9)**

CENTRAL TRUTH: The truly intelligent believer seeks to do things God's way, rather than their own way!

ADDITIONAL VERSES: Proverbs 14:12; John 16:23; 2 Corinthians 5:7

It is an intelligent choice to ask God's way. If Jesus says don't ask Him, but ask the Father in His name, then you should not ask Jesus, but rather ask the Father in Jesus' name. If God says to ask Him based upon His revealed will in the Logos or written Word of God, or in line with a Rhema Word that you have received from the Spirit of God, then ask according to God's will, with thanksgiving. Once you have done it God's way don't judge it according to how you feel. Judge it according to what the Word of God says. If the Word of God says you have the petition that you asked for, then you have it.

When you walk by faith, you have to divorce yourself from your feelings. That is difficult for people who grew up in churches where they were taught to conduct their relationship with God based upon the way they feel. Many denominations teach that you shouldn't have a religion that you can't feel sometimes. This conditions their people to judge their relationship with God and whether they have received an answer to their prayers based upon how they feel. However it is impossible to walk by faith and to walk by feelings at the same time. As Christians we are to walk by faith and not by sight or by sensory perception, such as feelings.

Keys to Formulating a Prayer of Faith:

1. Find Scriptures that promise you what you want from God;

2. Verbalize your petition;

3. Ask the Father in the Name of Jesus;

4. Let your asking be coupled with thanksgiving after you have prayed.

FAITH CONFESSION:
Whatever qualified desire I ask the Father for, in Jesus' name, He will give it to me.

WEEK 2
The Regimen of Faith – Component 1: <u>A</u>sking
Day 14
When You Ask, You Must See Yourself with the Answer

This is the confidence that we have in Him that if we ask anything according to His will He hears us and if we know that He hears us we know that we have the things that we desire of Him **(1 John 5-14-15)**.

CENTRAL TRUTH: By Continually Looking at the Word, Faith Sees the Answer.

ADDITIONAL VERSES: **Proverbs 4:20-22; Hebrews 12:1; Proverbs 4:20-22; Matthew 8:17**

In our past lessons we have been learning that faith is not so much something that we have, as much as it is something to do. In this lesson we will see that faith is not hoping that we will see the answer in the future, faith is seeing that we have the answer now. In 1 John the Scriptures says, once we have asked according to God's will (or God's Word), God's way, then we know that God hears us and we know that we have the things we desire.

In studying this word, know, I found that the Greek word translated know is: "eido". According to the Strong's Hebrew and Greek Dictionary and Thayer's Greek Definitions this word means properly, to see. So what the Apostle John was telling us is that after we ask God's way, we are to begin to see ourselves with the answer or the thing that we have asked for.

Too many people pray and pray, but they never see themselves with the answer. They see everything getting worse. They keep looking at the wrong thing – at the symptoms, at the circumstances, at themselves – and so they walk in unbelief and destroy the effects of their asking. You must get your mind on the answer. You must begin to see yourself as having already received what you prayed for. Constantly affirm, even in the face of contradictory evidence, that God has heard your prayer just because God's Word says He did.

How does one get their mind focused on the answer and not on the circumstances? In the book of Proverbs, the Bible says, "My son, give attention to my words; incline your ear to my sayings. Do not let them depart from your eyes; keep them in the midst of your heart; for they are life to those who find them, and health to all their flesh.

Notice here that the Bible says, "Let them (God's Words) not depart from your eyes..." Many people fail because they see themselves failing. If they are sick, they think of themselves as dying. God's Word says, "Himself (Jesus) took our infirmities, and bore our sickness..." If this verse of Scripture does not depart from before your eyes, you are bound to see yourself healed. However, if you do not see yourself as without sickness, then you have allowed that Word to depart from before your eyes. And even though God wants you well, He cannot do anything because you are not acting consistent with God's Word.

ASSIGNMENTS

1. Familiarize yourself with the Scriptures from this week's lessons that encourage you to Ask God for Things.

2. Complete the study questions from week two.

3. Attend Church on Sunday and a Family Life Cell Group next week.

1. What does the Scriptures say about the need to be instructed I faith?

2. What is the textbook for faith? _____

3. What is the established order of God?

4. What is the dismantling of erroneous thinking?

5. What is the assimilation of God's truth into our thinking? _____

6. What is seeing God's Word in a systematic way called?

7. What are the things that you can expect to operate with your faith during the manifestation of the faith process?

_____

_____

_____

_____

_____

_____

8. What is the divinely motivated assistance of others using their power on your behalf called?

_____

9. What specific Scripture did we use in this study to base the term "The Prayer of Petition"?

_____

_____

_____

_____

10. What are the rules for a petition prayer?

_____

_____

_____

_____

_____

11. Define Logos.

_____

_____

12. Define Rhema

_____

_____

13. What should you do to formulate a prayer of faith?

_____

_____

_____

_____

_____

_____

_____

14.   How do you see yourself with the answer to your prayer?

_____

_____

_____

Week No. 3
The Faith Regimen - Component 2: Believing

"Jesus said unto him, If you can believe, all things are possible to him that believes". **(Mark 9:23)**

CENTRAL TRUTH: The possibilities of your life are determined by your capacity to believe!

ADDITIONAL VERSES: Mark 11:23-24; Matthew 13:54-58; Mark 16:15-20; Acts 5:12-16; Numbers 23:19; Tutus 1:1-2

So far we have seen that faith can be defined as believing and acting like the Word of God is true. When this is in place, faith then allows the believer to tap into the supernatural power of God made available to His children whereby we can transform conditions, circumstances and situations in our lives in a manner that is consistent with the revealed will of God contained in the Word of God! This week we will look at the 2nd component of faith, which is believing. Believing is the essential component of faith that all of the other components depend upon. Each component of faith is vital and must be implemented properly in order for your faith to produce in a manner that is consistent with the promises of God. It is the believing component that separates the men from the boys and the women from the girls, so to speak. It is possible to do all of the other components of faith, without this component of believing, and nothing will happen because believing is the power behind your faith. Believing is the active ingredient to your faith.

The Scriptures reveal that believing is very important to our faith for several reasons. One of those reasons is found here in Mark 9:23. This is one of those life-changing passages that define the possibilities of a believer's life. The extent of the possibilities for your life is not determined by what others have done or by what others are doing. The extent of the possibilities of your life is determined by your ability or capacity to believe God's Word. When you understand this and begin to live your life based upon this understanding then the only thing that will stand between you defining something that is possible for you is the degree in which you develop your faith. According to Jesus, ***if you can believe, then anything is possible for you***. This means that it is possible for you to come out of poverty and lack into wealth and abundance. It is possible for you to come out of sickness and disease (regardless of your age or how long you have had your condition) into healing and supernatural health. You can come out of fear into faith, hatred into love, depression into joy and sadness into happiness if only you can and will believe!

Another powerful reason for believing is found in Mark 11. In vs. 24, the Word of God says that our faith will not work unless it contains the element of heart belief. In order for the prayer of faith to obtain the desired results, you and I must believe we have received at the moment that our prayer is offered to God...not the next day or at some other later time. Why, because believing is the active element of faith that reaches into the unrealities of hope and brings them into this natural realm!

In Matthew's gospel, we find that the one thing that stopped Jesus in His ministry to the sick was unbelief. Unbelief is the opposite of faith. In the Greek language from which the Bible was translated from, the Greek word for belief is pistia. The Greek word for unbelief is apistia. The "a" before pistia means, negative belief. It doesn't mean that you don't believe anything at all. It means you believe opposite from the Word of God. That is what unbelief is. I have heard scores of people say: "I don't believe that a man can 'lay his hands' on someone and they will be healed". Well this is directly opposite of what Jesus said and the book of Acts demonstrates. So that person still has a firm belief but it is opposite the Word of God, thus they will never obtain that which the Bible says that they can have. Therefore understanding the importance of believing and knowing the devastating results of unbelief should cause you to do everything that the Bible says you should do in order master the subject of faith and develop your faith to the highest level possible.

To believe is to accept something as being factual. This is always a function of the human will. Therefore you are in control of whether you will believe something or not, whether you will accept something as being factual or not. In John 20, the Apostle Thomas stated to the other Apostles around him that unless a certain set of criteria was met by either them or Jesus, he would not believe. He said that he had to see holes from the nails in Jesus' hands and be able to thrust his hand into Jesus side before he would even consider believing. Therefore we could say that Thomas' criteria for faith was all based on what I call "sense realm" evidence. Sense realm refers to that which can be detected through hearing, seeing, touching, smelling or tasting. When we first begin our faith journey, all of us have our capacity for believing limited by our sense realm perception of reality.

However, we must establish new criteria for believing that is beyond what I call sense realm evidence or sense realm knowledge. This new criteria must be the Word of God alone. When Jesus finally appeared to Thomas, He told Thomas two important things:

First He said: "Thomas, stop being faithless (or unbelieving), and start believing". Thus Jesus showed us that believing is an act of the human will.

Second He said: "Thomas, because you have seen... you have believed: (but) blessed are they that have not seen, and yet believe". Thus informing us that there is another criterion that can be established by which we can set our will to believe.

So biblical believing is to accept the Word of God as a fact without having any sense realm evidence to go along with what we believe. Instead of sense realm evidence, the character and integrity of God becomes the evidence for what we believe. In Hebrews 11:1, the Bible says that faith is the evidence of things not seen. Well faith comes by hearing and hearing by the Word of God, so the Word of God is all the evidence that we need to operate in the arena called faith!

FAITH CONFESSION:
God is not a liar, therefore I believe God's Word!

For by him (God) were all things crated, that are in heaven, and that are in earth VISIBLE and INVISIBLE...all things were created by Him and for Him:" **(Colossians 1:16)**

CENTRAL TRUTH: You must learn to see in the unseen realm to believe God in the face of overwhelming circumstances.

ADDITIONAL VERSES: 2 Kings 6:8-17; 2 Corinthians 5:7; 4:18; Hebrews 11:1,3; Romans 10:17; Ephesians 1:3; 2 Peter 1:2-4

Most of us grew up without having any knowledge of the impact of the unseen realm on the visible realm. We understood that God is invisible and heaven is invisible, but we really have not taken into account the real impact of the invisible realm or the spirit world on the seen world. Neither did we give much thought to our ability to interface with this realm. But we are spirit beings who live inside of physical bodies. Through our physical bodies we interface with this natural realm. However our spirits (or that invisible part of us) allow us to contact and transact business in this invisible realm or the realm of the spirit.

In the above verse in Colossians we are informed that in addition to the visible realm or visible world that we operate in 24/7, there is an INVISIBLE realm or world, which God Himself created. This invisible realm co-exists side by side or simultaneously with the natural or visible realm. In order for you to maximize your capacity to believe, you must learn to live with the thought of this invisible realm being a present reality, rather than only as a place you go to when you die. In the book of 2 Kings the prophet Elijah was surrounded by the Syrian army who wished to capture him. He had a young man with him who began to panic at the sight of the Syrian army, but Elijah assured the young man that there were actually more with them than the army that he saw right in front of him. Then Elisha prayed that God would allow the young man to see into the realm of the spirit and the young man saw that the mountain was full of horses and chariots of fire all around him and Elisha. The truth that we must understand from this is that this angelic army was there all the time! Elisha lived with this consciousness, so he was totally unmoved by what he saw in the natural realm. This also taught the young man to operate on a dimension of believing as Elisha did from then on. We can learn the same lesson from this incident.

Most of us have been taught that if we can't see it we are not to believe; however the Bible says that we walk by faith and not by sight. Bible faith or the God kind of faith is believing and acting like God's Word is true. This is true because the invisible realm is more reliable than the visible realm. It says that the things which are not seen are eternal, whereas the things which are seen are temporal (temporary or subject to change). In the book of Hebrews we find that all visible things here on earth (things which are subject to change) were made from these invisible things. God framed the world with His Word and the things that we see here were made from something that was once invisible.

As a believer, we have already discovered the power of the Word of God, when we acted on it to receive Christ as our Lord and Savior. We experienced it again when we received the baptism of the Holy Spirit, with the evidence of speaking in other tongues. So we have already begun to value the Word of God as being true. Well the Word of God tells us that there is this unseen realm, so we don't have to accept that there is this unseen realm just as "a leap of faith". We have proof of this invisible realm based on our past results from believing the Word of God. The Bible itself becomes our catalogue, which indexes and reveals to us those things that are available to us from this invisible realm. Just as you would order something from a Spiegel's catalogue or off a web page from the internet, without actually seeing the item, so we can "order up" so to speak, things that God has promised us from the Word of God!

The Apostle Paul understood that God has actually blessed us or provided for us everything that we need. The Apostle Peter told us this same thing and added that by the promises of God contained in Scripture, we can actually partake of or obtain all of these things. It is through believing these promises that we reach into the spirit realm and pull them into this natural realm.

FAITH CONFESSION:

I'm not moved by what I see or don't see...I believe God!

_____

"And Simon Peter answered and said, You are the Christ, the Son of the living God". **(Matthew 16:16)**

CENTRAL TRUTH: There is a difference between natural human faith and the God kind of faith.

ADDITIONAL VERSES: 2 Corinthians 4:18

Biblical believing in principle is to accept as fact that for which you have no sense realm evidence, solely because God's Word says it is true. You have spiritual evidence that it is true, but you do not have any sense realm evidence that it is true. If you have sense realm evidence, you don't have to *believe* it. You would *know* it. You should know it because you can verify it with one or more of your five physical senses. For every situation, there is God's (the spiritual) perspective and man's (the natural) perspective. Faith is choosing to look at things from God's perspective and then to believe and act like what God's Word says is so.

In our above scriptural reference, we see Jesus asking a question of Peter and the other disciples about who people thought He (Jesus) was and who they (the disciples) thought Jesus was. The people gave a natural perspective of who they thought Jesus was...a prophet or simply a great religious teacher or prophet similar to one from the past. Some even thought Jesus was the reincarnated version of one of these men. However the Apostle Peter stepped forward with God's perspective by saying, "You are the Christ (the Anointed King), the Son of the living God". Jesus informed Peter that this knowledge was not natural knowledge, but knowledge revealed or imparted to him from God Himself. Peter could have answered Him by saying, "Why you are the son of Joseph and Mary". That would have been the correct answer from the natural perspective. But Peter answered Jesus from a spiritual perspective.

To walk by faith and to believe, you must be able to look at things from God's perspective. You are not in the state of denial, even though you deny what you see in the natural to dictate the terms and conditions of your life. You are simply allowing the spiritual perspective to dictate the terms and conditions of your life. Here the Word of God instructs us not to look at what we see in the natural, but to focus on the things that are not seen.

I want to share something that the Holy Spirit revealed to me. In the life of a great king of Judah, named Jehoshaphat, the Bible tells us that he came to the prophet Elisha because his army was about to go into battle but they had run out of water. The prophet said that God would fill the valley with water and give him the victory in battle. Then the prophet said, this is a simple thing in the sight of God. Then I saw where King Asa, when facing 3 to 1 odds in another battle, prayed and said to the Lord, this is simple or easy for you to do O Lord. One day as I was studying this, the Holy Spirit spoke to me and said that the reason that so many Christians have difficulty believing for

Him to do great things in their lives is because they are looking at things only from the natural perspective.

You see to them the thing that they are believing for looks like it is so big to receive or requires such a big miracle or a large degree of faith to receive. However, if they would get the perspective that Elisha and that King Asa had, then believing would be so much easier. It doesn't matter how great the odds are that you are facing or how large a miracle you need, it is a simple matter in the sight of God. Begin to think about how God has made everything. In John 16, the Bible says that whatever we ask the Father God in Jesus' name, He will give it to us. The late Dr. P. C. Nelson, the leading Greek Scholar of his day, pointed out that the Greek word used there also carries with it the meaning of to make. Dr. Nelson went on to say that reading this from the literal Greek you could translate it as, "Whatever you ask the Father for in My name, He will give it to you; and if He doesn't have it He will <u>MAKE</u> it for you".

Biblical believing is not an act of denial, but a purposeful act of choosing to look at things from God's perspective. On days 19 and 20 we will talk about biblical meditation and how to change your perspective from a natural human perspective to God's perspective. This will enable you to expand your capacity to believe and receive. Then you can live on a much a higher plane of existence. Glory to God!

FAITH CONFESSION:

I possess the God kind of faith.

⁶And now, just as you accepted Christ Jesus as your Lord, you must continue to follow Him. ⁷Let your roots grow down into Him, and let your lives be built on Him. Then your faith will grow strong in the truth you were taught, and you will overflow with thankfulness. **Colossians 2:6-7 (NLT)**

CENTRAL TRUTH: By feeding on the Word of God, You can develop strong faith roots.

ADDITIONAL VERSES: 2 Thessalonians 1:3; Ephesians 3:20; Genesis 12:1-3; 2 Corinthians 5:7; Romans 10:17; Matthew 13:18-23; Mark 4:20; Luke 8:15

The Bible tells us that our faith can grow and grow exceedingly. Well the main component of faith is our capacity to believe. So obviously this would mean that we can expand our capacity to believe. For the rest of this week we will show you how to expand your capacity to believe so that you can rise to new levels of receiving from God. You must understand that God wants to do in our lives some things that are "...exceedingly, abundantly above all we can ask or think to ask..."

However God has determined that the methodology whereby His children would receive from Him is through faith, which means believing and acting on the Word of God or believing and acting like God's Word is true in our lives. God promised the great patriarch Abram or Abraham (and his descendants) prosperity, longevity of life, natural and spiritual descendants and the land of Canaan. But, God had to teach Abraham how to walk by faith before He could bless Abraham. God has promised to do the same things and more in your life, but you must learn to walk by faith in order to receive what God desires to do in your life. The great thing about this is that when properly instructed, the faith process actually becomes easy rather than hard.

In today's lesson we will look at the importance of the Word of God to expanding your faith. Romans chapter 10 says, "...faith comes by hearing and hearing by the Word of God". Jesus declared that the Word of God is like a seed. You must allow the Word of God to take root on the inside of you...in your heart, so that you can grow strong faith. Successful believing occurs based on the Word of God taking root inside of your heart. I want to share with you three things that allow for this:

First, you must properly UNDERSTAND the Word of God on the particular subject you are believing for. In Matthew chapter 13, the Lord Jesus Christ said:

¹⁸"Therefore hear the parable of the sower: ¹⁹When anyone hears the word of the kingdom, and does not understand *it,* then the wicked *one* comes and snatches away what was sown in his heart. This is he who received seed by the wayside. ²⁰But he who received the seed on stony places, this is he who hears the word and immediately receives it with joy; ²¹yet he has no root in himself, but endures only for a while. For when tribulation or persecution arises because of the word, immediately he stumbles. ²²Now he who received seed among the thorns is he who hears the word, and the cares

of this world and the deceitfulness of riches choke the word, and he becomes unfruitful. [23]But he who received seed on the good ground is he who hears the word and understands it, who indeed bears fruit and produces: some a hundredfold, some sixty, some thirty."

This particular parable is mentioned in all three of the "synoptic" gospels (or Matthew, Mark & Luke). Synoptic just means the gospels that give an account of the life of Jesus from the same point of view. The gospel of John was written from and entirely different point of view, and thus gives us many different stories and incidents in the life of Jesus that are not recorded in the synoptic gospels. We will look at one important point in each of these synoptic accounts for clarity of understanding of how to properly treat the Word of God in our faith development process.

Here in Matthew's gospel, we are told that the first thing that we must do if we want to be able to believe the Word of God is that we must UNDERSTAND it. The Word for understand means, "...to *put together*, (mentally), that is, to *comprehend* (according to the Strong's Concordance). Thayer's Greek Definitions defines this word as: "...to put (as it were) the perception with the thing perceived; to set or join together in the mind". So it is important that you stay with the Word until you actually mentally comprehend it. God doesn't expect you to check your mind at the door when it comes to faith. God expects you to study until you understand it. The Bible says that we are to study to show ourselves approved in the things of God. So it is very important that you sit up under a good Bible teaching ministry like Calvary Fellowship International church, and then take what you are taught and go back home and study it. This will necessitate you going out and purchasing at least three valuable study tools, which are The Strong's Exhaustive Concordance of the Bible, W. E. Vines Expository Dictionary of Old and New Testament Words and The Amplified Version of the Bible. These are very basic study tools that will help you to study the meaning of the original Hebrew and Greek Words in the Bible so that you can get a better understanding of what the Word is saying.

Second, in the 4th Chapter of Mark's gospel we are told that we must properly accept or EMBRACE the Word of God.   This word "accept" means, "to embrace or delight in" according to Strong's. Thayer's adds to it the meanings of, "to take up, take upon one's self; to admit, i.e. not to reject, to accept; to acknowledge as one's own". If you want to increase your capacity to believe, you must begin to delight in reading and studying the Word of God. You must begin to accept what it says as if it applies to you personally. You must acknowledge it as your own, or as if God is talking directly to you through the Word.

Finally, you must properly RETAIN the Word. In Luke 8, the Bible says that those who having heard the Word...KEEP it and bear fruit..." the Word keep means to hold fast to, to keep in memory, to possess, to retain, seize on. It means to keep secure, to keep firm possession of to get possession of. This simply means that you must not let the Word slip from your heart, your mind or your memory if you want the Word of God to produce the promised results in your life.

FAITH CONFESSION:

My faith is rooted and grounded in God's Word!

"And the Apostles said to the Lord, 'Increase our faith'". **Luke 17:5**

CENTRAL TRUTH: Understanding the power of biblical meditation.

ADDITIONAL VERSES:

It is vital that you understand that your belief system has been formulated by four controllable elements. These elements are:

1. The Influential People in your life who talk to you and help to shape your thinking;

2. The Information that is gained through repetitions learning;

3. The Environment in which you were brought up in and live in today;

4. The Experiences of your life that made a lasting impact on you.

In order for us to elevate our belief system from the low level of sense realm knowledge and experiences, it is critical to understand how to impact these four controllable areas in such a way that we rise above our prior conditioning, so we can walk on a higher plane of living. God has given us instructions that will change these four areas of influence over our belief system.

First, God tells us to come out from among our environment **(2 Corinthians 6:17).** That is what He told Abram, who later became Abraham. God said, Abram, I can't bless you here. You have to leave your county, your kindred and your father's house, and go to a land that I will show you. The Bible tells us that Abraham's family members were idol worshippers and God needed to get him out of that environment so that He could teach him how to serve Him.

Second, God changes our influential authority figure **(Psalms 138:2)**, by telling us to make His Word the final authority in our lives. God said, I have magnified My Word even above My name. By saying that, God is telling us that there is no other authority on earth higher than His Word.

Third, God tells us to begin to hear His Word on a repetitious basis **(Psalms 1:1-3)**. We are told to mediate on the Word of God day and night. That calls for us to change our thinking about the Bible. Most believers just see the Bible as the good book. It is more than the good book; it is the final authority for everything that we are to believe relative to our life in God.

The strength of our faith rests in our capacity to believe. Therefore, we can never expand beyond that for which we can believe. If you want to expand in life, then you must expand your capacity to believe.

Mark 11:23 says, "...Whosoever shall SAY unto this mountain, be thou removed, and be thou cast into the sea, and shall not doubt in his heart but shall BELIEVE that those things, which he SAITH shall come to pass, he shall have whatsoever he SAITH." Believing sits right in the middle of all of this. It is the anchor to our faith. You can start talking and confessing things, but if you don't believe it, there will be no manifestation. <u>Therefore it would behoove you to spend more time working on the believing component of your faith so that you can expand or raise your level of believing and therefore receiving.</u> The confession component will also work more effectively. In fact, the Bible says, "...out of the abundance of the heart the mouth speaks" and "...we having the same spirit of faith BELIEVE, and therefore SPEAK". In other words, it's easier to speak it when your heart is full of belief. Speaking then becomes almost automatic. Then, when you confess it out of a believing heart, it will take a lot less time for you to receive the manifestation of your faith.

Finally, God tells us the importance of creating new experiences **(Romans 5:3-4)**. Experiences produce hope because experiences make the most potent impact on what we believe. They are very important and give us a greater sense of expectation for the future.

Each of these elements impacts our belief system and are controllable. This means that with work, we can expand our capacity to believe!

FAITH CONFESSION:

When I speak to my circumstances they must change because Jesus said they would!

"This book of the law shall not depart from you mouth, but you shall meditate in it day and night, that you may observe to do according to all that is written in it. For then you will make your way prosperous and then you will have good success". **Joshua 1:8**

CENTRAL TRUTH: Through Biblical Meditation it's possible to expand your capacity to believe.

ADDITIONAL VERSES: Psalm 1:3; 1Timothy 4:15; Philippians 4:8; Psalm 45:1; Genesis 30:37-38; 31:10-12; Colossians 3:2

Meditation is the method that God has provided so that you and I can expand our capacity to believe! He who does not spend time meditating upon the Word of God is not serious about expanding their capacity to believe. In the book of Psalms, Ch. 1, we are told that the result of meditation is that we shall be like a tree planted by the rivers of water, that brings forth his fruit in his season; his leaf also shall not wither, and whatever he does shall PROSPER!

The Apostle Paul told his spiritual son Timothy to meditate on the things that he wrote to him about because by so doing, it would cause him to profit in life and ministry. Paul also told the Philippians to meditate on things that are noble, just pure, lovely, of a good report, virtuous and praiseworthy. So we can see that the principle of meditation can be found in both the Old and New Testaments.

The Hebrew word for meditation carries with it a three-fold meaning that we can see clearly in Joshua. First it means to ponder or think about over and over again. Then it also means to speak to ones' self. Finally it means to imagine or visualize.

Biblical meditation works like an internal commercial on the canvas of your imagination giving you an imagined experience that strongly impacts what you believe. Remember that an experience has a more potent impact on what you believe than anything else.

An experience is made up of words, emotions and images (or pictures). Images can be seen on the canvas of your imagination on a repetitious basis when meditating. You have an internal video camera in your imagination that allows you to play and re-play experiences over and over again. This camera allows you to either play images of your past called memories or images of your future, which the Bible calls meditation. Memories are a good thing, but they can keep you living for and in the past, while meditation helps you to shape your preferred future. The choice is your. You can be trapped; living in the memories of a bad past, or freed through meditation to live in a better future.

Your belief system does not readily distinguish between something that is vividly imagined and something that you actually go through. You have experienced this in some of your dreams and nightmares that you have had.

You can expand your capacity to believe by looking at your future on the canvas of your imagination, seeing yourself in possession of the things for which God has promised and that you are believing for, as if you were already enjoying them! All of these things can be verified in Word of God as we examine the principles of faith that God taught His people. We can see how this impacted Abraham's faith in Genesis 15:4-6. We see that it impacted the children of Israel's faith in Numbers 21:4-9. And finally, we see that it impacted Ezekiel's faith in Ezekiel 37:1-14. Ezekiel's belief system was impacted and he could go forward with confidence and faith to deliver God's message to Israel and believe that it would happen!

Meditation involves each of these components:

1. **Verbalization** – the speaking of the promise(s) of God so as to create images on your heart (Psalm 45:1)

2 **Visualization** – the purposeful playing of these images in your heart through visual association (Genesis 30:37-38; 31:10-12);

3 **Simulation** – the acting out of what you visualize on the level where you are. This may mean dressing for success. This may mean cleaning out your garage for that new car. But you prepare for it on the level where you are to the best of your ability.

4 **Saturation** – this is doing the first three steps over and over… again and again until your belief system has been saturated with faith so that it lines up with what God has promised you.

FAITH CONFESSION:

Because I see myself with it, I can believe it and therefore I will have it.

[11]And we desire that each one of you ...imitate those who through faith and patience inherit the promises. [13]For when God made a promise to Abraham, because He could swear by no one greater, He swore by Himself, [14]saying, *"Surely blessing I will bless you, and multiplying I will multiply you."* [15]And so, after he had patiently endured, he obtained the promise. **Hebrews 6:11-15 (NKJV)**

CENTRAL TRUTH: Your capacity to believe can be expanded through diligent effort.

ADDITIONAL VERSES: Hebrews 11:6; James 1:6-8; Genesis 13:14-17 (NLT); Genesis 12:1-3; Genesis 15:5-6; Galatians 3:7, 9; Ezekiel 37:1-14

God made a promise to bless Abram or Abraham. He couldn't bless him unless Abraham operated in faith because without faith, it is impossible to please God, and without faith, no one can expect to receive anything from the Lord. It is the order of God for mankind to receive from Him by faith.

In the book of Genesis we see how God continually worked with Abraham to expand his capacity to believe. First, in the 13th Chapter of Genesis we see that after Abram and his nephew Lot separated from each other, the LORD challenged Abram to: "**Look** <u>as far as you can see in every direction</u>—north and south, east and west. I am giving all this land, as far as you can see, to you and your descendants as a permanent possession. [16]And I will give you so many descendants that, like the dust of the earth, they cannot be counted! [17]Go and **walk** <u>through the land in every direction,</u> for I am giving it to you."

What we see God doing is taking Abraham through a couple of the steps of Biblical meditation. In verse 14, God said, "look". The New King James version says, "Lift up your eyes now and look..." Even though God wanted to bless Abraham, he had to get Abraham to change the perspective of his situation and get him to see what God had for him. God had already promised this land to Abraham, but Abraham had to begin to see himself and his descendants possessing it because it was still in the hands of the Canaanites. This is VISUALIZATION. Then in verse 16, God told Abraham to walk through the land in every direction. This is SIMULATION. We will see later on that God also used VERBALIZATION, when he changed Abram's name to Abraham (or the father of many nations). Then SATURATION is in operation each time Abraham referred to himself as the father of many nations, as he addressed others and as others called out to him by name as Abraham. We will address verbalization all through next week.

In Chapter 15 of Genesis we see a second example of God working with Abraham to expand his capacity to believe. In verses 5 and 6, the Bibles says,

[5]Then (God) brought (Abram) outside and said, "<u>Look</u> now toward heaven, and count the stars if you are able to number them." And He said to him, "So shall your descendants be." [6]And he <u>believed</u> in the LORD, and He accounted it to him for righteousness.

Again the Bible shows us that through visualizing what God had promised him, Abraham was able to expand his capacity to believe and therefore receive what God had promised him. The reason that this is important to you and me is because the book of Galatians says that "...those who are of faith are sons of Abraham..." "...Those who *are* of faith are blessed with **believing** Abraham..." Even though God promised to bless Abram or Abraham, He had to walk Abraham through the faith development process before Abraham could receive what God wanted to do for him. It is the same way in our lives.

As I said earlier, though God had promised to bless Abraham He couldn't bless Abraham until Abraham operated in true Bible faith, or the God kind of faith. Therefore God had to systematically teach him the principles that I am teaching you. God taught Abraham how to meditate.

God did the same thing with Ezekiel. God wanted to impact Ezekiel so that he could preach a message of unity. He gave him this awesome vision of preaching in the valley of dry bones. After the vision, he tells Ezekiel to go tell my people that I can bring them together. After seeing this massive vision of these bones coming together and standing as an army, Ezekiel's belief system was impacted and he could go forward with confidence and faith to see it happen.

When you are standing in faith for something, you need to spend time meditating – seeing yourself with it. You need to support that meditation with some external props; such as pictures or a model of the item you are believing for and visit it often. This is the way to work on expanding your capacity to believe and receive it.

ASSIGNMENTS

1. Familiarize yourself with the Faith Scriptures from this week's lessons.

2. Complete the study questions from week one.

3. Attend Church on Sunday and a Family Life Cell Group next week.

FAITH CONFESSION:

Today I will raise my level of faith through seeing myself with what God promised me.

1. Name thee reasons why the believing component is important.

_____

_____

_____

_____

Unbelief restricts the impact of the power of God in your life.

☐ TRUE   ☐ FALSE

We must establish new criteria for believing other than the sense realm.

☐ TRUE   ☐ FALSE

Define biblical believing.

_____

Fill in the blank: The _____ itself becomes our catalogue, which indexes and reveals to us those things that are available to us from this invisible realm.

Which of the following is more real? Circle one

      A. The visible world (or)   B. The invisible world

The world was made with which of the following?

    a. Things that are visible

    b. Things that are invisible

For every situation there are two perspectives. What are they?

_____

What doses sense realm evidence mean.

_____

Name the controllable elements that impact our belief system.

_____

_____

_____

_____

_____

What four areas in meditation affect our belief system?

_____

_____

_____

_____

Which of the following has the most potent impact on what you believe

- Credible others

- Repetitious information

- An experience

- None of the above

Week No. 4
The Faith Regimen - Component 3: Confessing

"For with the heart man believes to righteousness and with the MOUTH <u>confession</u> is made unto salvation". **(Romans 10:10)**

CENTRAL TRUTH: By confessing the Lordship of Jesus Christ, one is born again.

ADDITIONAL VERSES: 1 John 1:9; John 16:7-11; Romans 10:9-10, 13; Matthew 10:32-33

Last week we looked at the first part of this verse, which deals with believing with the heart. This week we will study the importance of biblical confession. Due to a limited view of confession, most Christians hear this word and immediately think of confessing sins to a priest. There is something to confessing our sins, but the Bible never said we *had to* confess our sins to a priest or a minister in order to be forgiven. We can confess our sins directly to God and receive forgiveness of our sins. But this is just one side of the coin called confession...the negative side. But there is another side to confession, the positive side, which we will be addressing this week.

The dictionary says that to confess means "to make confession of one's faults", but it also means, "to acknowledge or to own, to acknowledge faith in". Actually, there are three primary kinds of confession spoken of in the New Testament: (1) The Unsaved Person's confession of faith in the Lordship of Jesus Christ and His resurrection from the dead that causes a person to become a child of God; (2) The Christian's confession of his or her sins when we disobey the Word or the Spirit of God in order to restore fellowship and (3) The confession of our faith in the Word of God and our rights and privileges in Christ.

In the 16th Chapter of the gospel of John, He records Jesus saying that the Holy Spirit will convict the world of sin. This sin is that the world (or the unsaved person) doesn't believe on Him. This is the only sin that the Holy Spirit is assigned to convict the world of. Yet we often hear even ministers tell people that they must confess all of the sins that they ever committed in order to be saved. But that's actually impossible. I know that before I became a Christian, there were things that I had done that the Bible calls sin, but I didn't even know they were sins, because I didn't know the Bible. And, even if I had known everything that the Bible declares is sin, I did so much sinning that there is no way that I could have remembered every sin that I had ever committed...and neither could anyone else for that matter.

So, an unsaved person couldn't possibly confess each and every one of their sins. In the Book of Romans, the Bible tells us exactly what the unsaved person is to confess. The unsaved are to "...confess with [their] mouth the [Lordship of] Jesus and believe in [their] heart that God has raised him from the dead..." Then they will be saved. In God's view, the unsaved person only has one sin standing in their way to salvation and that is their rejection of Jesus Christ as Savior and Lord. Yes, the unsaved person must repent of his or her sins, which means that they must be truly sorry for their past sins and turn away from them and acknowledging their need of a Savior. Then the unsaved person must let Jesus dominate their life daily. Confessing the Lordship of Jesus is the first step to all that God has for you.

In the 10th Chapter of the gospel of Matthew, the Lord Jesus said:

"Whoever confesses Me before men, him I will also confess before My Father who is in heaven. But whoever denies Me before men, him I will also deny before My Father who is in heaven". Therefore it is important for you to confess Jesus publicly before other people. This is the key to making a break with the world. By confessing Jesus publicly, you take your stand as a child of God. This immediately puts us under Christ's supervision, care and protection. Before this Satan was our Lord, but now Jesus is our Lord. This also lets Satan know that Jesus is your Lord and, by so doing, you overcome his hold on you and you gain the victory over the fear of being different when Satan tries to place that in your life to trap you in fear as a CIA or undercover Christian. Everybody else has come out the closet! You don't need to be afraid to come out of the closet as a Christian. Being a Christian is a good thing, glory to God!

FAITH CONFESSION:

Jesus died for my sins, rose from the dead and He is my Lord!

"For with the heart man believes to righteousness and with the MOUTH confession is made unto salvation". **(Romans 10:10)**

CENTRAL TRUTH: By confessing our sins, we restore broken fellowship with God.

ADDITIONAL VERSES: 1 John 1:3-10, Isaiah 43; 24; Jeremiah 31:34; Psalms 103:1-3

In 1 John we see the word "fellowship" mentioned several times throughout this passage. The Apostle John didn't write these verses to unsaved people; he wrote them to Christians. Unsaved people don't have fellowship (or relationship for that matter) with God. But we believers do. Until an unsaved person confesses Jesus Christ, he or she is out of relationship and fellowship with God. They are the creation of God, but not a child of God.

Whenever a Christian sins, they do not lose their relationship with God. We continue to be His children, but we break fellowship with God. Fellowship refers to the enjoyment that we have in our relationship with God. When a man and a woman get married, they become related to each other through marriage. They are legal relatives...they are actually, in the eyes of the law, "next of kin". So they have relationship. Now how the two of them get along is what the Bible is speaking of here when it talks about fellowship.

As I said, whenever a Christian sins, we break our fellowship with God. It is through the confession of said sins that we restore our fellowship with God. However if we say that we have not committed any sin and yet the fellowship is broken, then our faith will be weak and ineffective. But, if we will confess our sins, God will be faithful and just to forgive our sins, and to cleanse us from all unrighteousness. If you are a Christian whenever you sin, you will know it. If you don't know it, don't try to drag up something with which to condemn yourself. If you always look for something to condemn yourself, you will rob yourself of faith. If you sin though, the instant that you do, you will know it right on the inside of you. Your own spirit will instantly let you know that you have sinned. Whenever you sin, don't delay in confessing your sin and asking the Lord for His forgiveness. According to 1 John 1:9, He will definitely forgive you.

When you confess your sins, God forgives you at that moment and you stand, once again, in His presence as if you had never sinned. It is not necessary to keep confessing those same sins over and over again, for this builds weakness into your spirit through "sin consciousness. In the book of Isaiah, the Bible tells us that God blots out our sins and remembers them no more. Jeremiah also said that God would forgive our iniquity and remember our sins no more. Finally, in the 103rd Psalm, the Bible tells us that God will forgive all of our iniquities or every sin.

FAITH CONFESSION:

When I confess my sins, God is faithful and right to forgive me.

"For with the heart man believes to righteousness and with the MOUTH <u>confession</u> is made unto salvation". **(Romans 10:10)**

CENTRAL TRUTH: Confession is faith's way of expressing itself. Faith's confessions create a new biblical reality for our lives.

ADDITIONAL VERSES: 2 Corinthians 4:13; Mark 4:13-20, 26-29;

So far in our studies on confession we have addressed the negative side of confession, as it relates to the removal of sin. For the rest of the week we will discuss the confession of God's Word and the powerful results that it will produce, when done from a believing heart. We have defined faith as *believing* and *acting* like God's Word is true. Confessing God's Word involves both believing and acting like God's Word is so. The Scriptures say: "...we *believe* and therefore we *speak*".

An important component to the faith regimen is the confession of your faith. A faith confession is a statement that one chooses to make in agreement with God's Word, regardless of their situation, circumstances, or how bad or contrary things may appear. It is a quality decision to, not only believe but also to, speak in line with what God's Word says about your life over what your circumstances say. A faith confession is not a denial of the facts about your situation...it is a choice to believe and speak in line with God's Word in spite of your situation. You understand that you don't have any money if that is the case. You don't write hot checks, but you do choose to say what God says about your circumstances. He says that He will supply all of your needs according to His riches in glory by Christ Jesus. Therefore you then choose to say the same thing that God has said.

Faith isn't magic; it is a spiritual process that works in a progressive manner to bring about a new reality in one's life. The parable of the sower in the 4th Chapter of Mark shows us how the faith process works in a progressive manner. Jesus told us that the Word of God works as a seed works in the ground. The ground there in these verses refers to the heart or the spirit of man.

This parable shows us that we don't have to know how the manifestation is going to occur. But we have an expectation of God giving us a plan of action. Then we start off in faith, not knowing how the manifestation is going to come to pass. We don't try to figure it out. We leave the details of how it will occur up to God. He can do it any way He so chooses. Also, we see from Mark 4:26 that the manifestation may not necessarily occur over night. Instant results do sometimes occur, but we can't predict an instant manifestation. I don't know when it's going to occur, but I do know that it will occur because of my faith in God.

Confession of God's Word builds faith. Confession is affirming something we believe. It is testifying to something we know. It is witnessing for a truth that we have embraced. Our confession should be focused around six scriptural points:

1. What God in Christ has done for us in His great plan of redemption;

2. What God, through the Word and the Spirit of God, has done in us in the new birth and the baptism with the Holy Spirit;

3. What we are to God the Father in Christ Jesus.

4. What Jesus is doing for us now, at the right hand of the Father God, as He ever lives to make intercession for us.

5. What God can do through us, or what His Word can do through our lips;

6. What we can do through the name of Jesus and through the power of the Holy Spirit.

In I Timothy we are told that when we begin moving in faith we will have a fight on our hands. This fight is not with the devil; it is a fight with the thoughts that the devil will try to place in your mind to get you to back off from confessing the Word. However the Bible says that we are to hold fast to our confession of faith. The devil will also work through people to try to intimidate you into wavering over your confession of faith due to the length of time that it may take. Many believers become discouraged and stop confessing God's Word about the thing that they are believing for or they will start toning down their confession. Don't waver. Be bold! Remember, you don't have anything to lose if it doesn't work...the situation stays the same. But if it works, and it will work if you stay with the process, then you have everything to gain! You will reap in due season if you do not faint or loose heart. This is the discipline required for walking by faith. Don't give up when you are challenged. Just keep on saying what God's Word says about you and your circumstances.

FAITH CONFESSION:

My faith will move the mountains in my life!

It is the spirit who gives life; the flesh profits nothing. The words that I speak to you are spirit and they are life. **(John 6:63)**

CENTRAL TRUTH: You must understand the dynamic power of the spoken Word.

ADDITIONAL VERSES: Proverbs 18:21; Hebrews 11:3; Mark 11:23; Isaiah 41:10

You must recognize that your words are "containers". Words do more than communicate to others your thoughts and desires; words also release the spiritual life that comes from your spirit as you speak them. Jesus said that His words were spiritual containers that released life. The wise man Solomon tells us however that our words can either be carriers of death or containers of life.

The writer of Hebrews tells us that the reason that words are so important is because God created the physical universe through words, therefore this world responds to words. In Genesis, God said, "let there be..." over and over again. What He was displaying for us is that this planet responds to words. Whatever God said to "let there be", He saw that thing come to pass and God said it was good. Words are the spiritual containers that carried the power of God that brought forth the heavens and the earth.

Your words also have power! The Bible says that a man who believes that what he says shall come to pass; he will have what he says. You have to know that when you open your mouth and say something, things start happening in the invisible realm!

A wrong confession is a confession of defeat and failure and to the domination of the devil in one's life. I've heard of people saying, "Please pray for me...the devil's been after me all week; bless his holy name". They don't even realize or intend to bless the devil's name. They meant to bless God's name, but by constantly talking about what the devil is doing to hold them back and defeat them, that is exactly who they are praising. Speaking of how the devil is hindering you and keeping you from success...about how he is holding you in bondage...about how he is keeping you sick, is a confession of defeat. Such a confession simply glorifies the devil.

You see if your confession is wrong, it's because your believing is wrong. If your believing is wrong it is because your thinking is wrong. If your thinking is wrong, it is because your mind has not been renewed yet with the Word of God. Sometimes the teachings of the Word of God may not seem reasonable to your mind because your mind hasn't been renewed to the Word of God yet.

Instead of confessing your doubts and fears, confess what God's Word says. God said in Isaiah, "Fear thou not; for I am with you..." A good confession dispels fear. In Isaiah 41:10, we are told to fear not, because God is with us and He will strengthen us, help us and uphold us with His victorious right hand. Too many Christians are always running around talking about how fearful, weak and helpless they are. They always talk about how they are about to go down when trouble comes. But a good confession says, "God is with me." God is my strength and my helper and He is upholding me in His victorious right hand, so I will never go down to defeat! As you begin to talk like that <u>daily</u>, you will drive fear out of your life, in Jesus' name!

12Then (the angel Gabriel) said to me, "Do not fear, Daniel, for from the first day that you set your heart to understand, and to humble yourself before your God, your words were heard; and I have come because of your words. **Daniel 10:12 (NKJV)**

CENTRAL TRUTH: Your Confession works in two worlds.

ADDITIONAL VERSES: Psalms 103:20; Luke 10:17-20; Matthew 8:16; Luke 17:5-6;-11; James 3:8 Isaiah 53:5; 1 Peter 2:24; 1 Thessalonians 5:23Ecclesiastes 12:8

When we were growing up we were not taught the dynamic power of the spoken word. We were told: "sticks and stones may break my bones, but words will never hurt me". My mother taught me this in order to keep me from being concerned about things people said about me or to buttress any "name calling" that might occur between children. This leads to us thinking that words really don't matter. But the Word of God says that words do matter. As a spirit being yourself when you speak you make things happen in the spiritual realm. Today we are going to look at several things that are affected by our confession of God's Word.

First, we find in our foundation verse that angels are dispatched in response to the words of human beings. In the 103 Psalm, we find that angels hearken or heed the voice of God's Word. Notice that it doesn't say God's voice, but the voice of God's Word. When we confess or voice God's Word, angels hearken, heed or listen to it just like they listen to God Himself.

Second, we can see that demonic forces are restrained when you speak God's Word and use the name of Jesus. In Luke 10, the Bible says that the Apostles came to Jesus elated over how demons were subject to them through speaking and using the name of Jesus. You and I are able to exercise authority over the devil with the words of our mouth. Jesus Himself cast out evil spirits with a word. Also in Matthew 4, when Jesus was involved in spiritual combat face to face with the devil, Jesus quoted the Word of God to defeat Satan.

Third, Jesus told us in Luke 17 that you can speak faith filled words to an object and it will obey you. Faith is a spiritual force, carried or contained in words. Though faith is invisible, it is real. The Word of God framed the worlds or ages. The force of faith causes things to obey you. Even as God formed the worlds with the words of His mouth, you have the ability to form your world with the words of your mouth. That is why the devil fights against the area of confession so much. Your words are like the fuse that lights the match of the powerful force of faith. Without speaking or releasing your faith through words, your faith will be inert, inactive or idle.

Fourth, we establish our hearts in faith with our words. The Book of James says that corrupt things and good things should not come out of the same fountain or spring. Therefore you have to guard the things that you say on an ongoing basis. You can't get caught up in mess and corrupt communication. This will foul up the power of your words to work on your behalf with something good. So, it is important for you to build yourself up to believe by speaking God's Word. In the book of Romans the Bible says, *"So then faith cometh by hearing, and hearing by the word of God"*. When you speak the Word, guess who also hears it? You hear it. Therefore you are building up your faith as you speak the Word, because you are causing faith to come.

When you confess the Word of God, it is like you are charging yourself or building yourself up. Faith comes by hearing and hearing by the Word of God. You may start off confessing the Word of God, speaking in agreement with God's Word, even though your believing may not be where it needs to be. But as you speak the Word, faith will come. Don't wait until your faith is fully developed to start declare what God's Word says about your situation because by speaking God's Word, even when you are struggling with believing, this helps you to believe it. Then, one day, you will say it out of a fully persuaded heart and things will start happening in this natural realm.

I remember when I had a painful growth that had developed under the skin on my left wrist. I had just quit my job at the telephone company in Los Angeles and moved all the way to Tulsa, OK to attend Bible College in Oklahoma. There I was working a minimum wage job for a fast food restaurant and I had no medical insurance. I went to the Word of God and found about 20 or 30 verses that addressed healing in the redemptive work of Christ. I began to meditate on those verses and confess them over my body. At the beginning, though I believed that God's Word was true, my heart was full of fear. The devil was telling me that I had cancer. But I began to confess God's Word, even though my believing was not where it should have been. After about two weeks of confessing the Word I realized the fear had departed from my heart. The Word began it's work inside of me, in my spirit, before its affects could be seen outside of me; in my body. (You see the real you and the real me is our spirit. Man [Homo sapiens] is a spirit, who lives in a body and possesses a soul. The word starts working in our spirit first.) Then after about two or three more weeks, the pain in my wrist had stopped, but the growth was still there. Finally, about a week later, I woke up one morning and looked at that growth and started laughing at it. I said, "You lying vanity you. I am not trying to be healed, I am already healed" and I laughed some more. Well by 5:30 that evening the growth was gone. Through feeding on the Word of God, meditating on it and confessing it, my heart was filled with faith so that I could receive what God had already declared was mine.

FAITH CONFESSION:

Sickness is a lying vanity because by Jesus' stripes I am healed.

WEEK 4
The Regimen of Faith – Component 4: <u>C</u>onfessing
Day 27
Characteristics of a Faith Confession

"God...calls those things which do not exist as though they did (exist)". **Romans 4:17**

CENTRAL TRUTH: If you don't begin to call yourself what God calls you, you will never become what God says that you are.

ADDITIONAL VERSES: Mark 11:22; John 17:17; 1 Peter 2:24; Philippians 4:15-19; Genesis 17:1-5; 15-16;

We have seen that the Lord Jesus told us that we are to have faith in God, or literally the faith of God or the God kind of faith. This means that our faith can and should operate consistent with the way that God operates His faith. Here in the book of Romans, we see that one thing involved in the way that God uses His faith is by calling those things that do not exist as though they did exist. There is a difference between calling those things that do not exist as though they do exist and calling those things that are as though they are not. God did not say that you were not sick. Therefore, if you say, "I am not sick", you are not properly acting on this principle. (This is a little tricky, but stay with me.) That is not a faith confession. It's not even a positive statement. You could simply be operating in denial.

A positive faith confession affirms what it believes; testifies to something it knows; witnesses to a truth that it has embraced. Well the Bible is truth. It declares that by His stripes you were healed. So a confession that calls those things that be not (that you are healed), as though they were (or as though you were already healed). So a good faith confession would say: "I believe that by His stripes I am healed". Though you don't have any sense realm evidence for this, you are choosing not only to believe, but to speak in line with the Word of God.

Again, Romans 4 says that God calls things that be not as though they were or as though they did exist. It doesn't tell us to call things that are as though they are not. In other Words it doesn't tell us to <u>deny</u> anything. It is telling us to <u>affirm</u> what we believe. Though very subtle, there is a major difference between these two types of confession. So don't say, "I am not broke". You are broke if you don't have any money. What you should say is, "Because I am a tither and a giver all of my needs are met according to God's riches in glory by Christ Jesus", as the book of Philippians tells us. (Note: we will address the part that giving plays in our faith for finances later on.) You should say that God meets all of my needs, according to His riches in glory, by Christ Jesus.

The Scriptures are replete with examples of how confession is the scriptural key that allows us to tap into the supernatural power of God to change circumstances, situations and conditions in our lives so that they become consistent with the will of God as revealed in the Scriptures. Even though the promise that God had for Abram was critical to the plan of God and the whole human race, God could not do it until Abram received it through faith. This should let us know that if God would not violate His order for Abram, he is not going to violate it for you or for me.

In Genesis 17, God changed Abram's name to Abraham to teach him the principle of calling those things that be not as though they were. The name Abraham means, "Father of many nations". Every time Abram heard his new name spoken by himself or someone else, he heard it in the present tense. He didn't hear "you who are going to be the father of a multitude or father of many nations", Abraham heard, "you are the father of many nations (now)"! When Abraham introduced himself, he said, "I am 'the father of many nations'" (because that is who God said that he was). Abraham was speaking in agreement with the Word of God. It is not a lie to choose, by an act of your will, to say what God's Word says about you or your situation. Here we have scriptural precedence for doing this.

To show that this is very powerful and important, later on in the same chapter, God would also change Abraham's wife's name from Sarai (which meant the princess) to Sarah, the mother of many. You see if you don't begin to say what God says you are before it occurs, then you will never become what God intends for you to be through faith. (You may get there some other way, like medical surgery or through winning the lottery or something, but not by faith. I don't advise that you relegate your future to the lottery when you can become wealthy by utilizing the principles of faith for prosperity. Though I support the fine work of medical doctors, there is a better way to receive healing, which is to receive healing by faith through the power of God. It doesn't leave a scar!) When Sarai began to call herself Sarah, she was both barren and too far advanced in age to have a child naturally. In fact Sarai laughed when she heard the news. She couldn't believe it at first. God had to get her to change her name so she would change her speaking. She had to begin to call herself the mother of many before she ever had one child born to her. When people asked here "where are your children, mother of many", she had to respond and say, "I am the mother of many because God said that I am". And I believe it, even though it hasn't occurred yet.

From this point on in Scripture you will never see Abraham (or anyone else) refer to himself as Abram and you will never see Sarah (or anyone else) refer to herself as Sarai. This shows you that you have to be persistent in calling yourself what God calls you or saying about yourself what God says about you. Can you call yourself blessed when all around you it doesn't look like you're blessed? Can you call yourself abundantly supplied when your needs have needs. You must be able to do this before you will ever become what God has said that you already are. You have to be disciplined enough to find out what God's Word says about you and then say the same thing about yourself. Your faith confession must be personal, present tense and persistent for it to prove to be productive in your life.

Heaven is already saying things about you, good things, in spite of what you or others are saying about you right now. God told Abram that He had already made him the father of many nations, several years prior to his name change. God and all heaven saw Abram this way. However until Abraham began to say about himself what heaven was already saying about him, nothing happened relative to he and Sarai having a child.

FAITH CONFESSION:
I am now everything that God and heaven is saying about me.

Therefore do not cast away your confidence, which has great reward. **(Hebrew 10:35 NKJV)**

CENTRAL THEME: You can develop confidence in your confession's power to bring things to pass.

Our foundation verse for today's lesson tells us that you have to have confidence in the power of your confession. Don't cast away or throw aside your confidence. Don't cast away the confession of your faith. Don't take it lightly. Don't stop speaking the Word. Don't allow anyone to intimidate you. The process will produce the promised results in your life.

How do you learn to be confident? Confidence is based on knowledge. If you are going to be confident in your confession, it will be based on the knowledge that you have. You need to know the following to have confidence in your confession:

1. You must know <u>who you are,</u> based on the Word of God.
2. You must know <u>what Satan can and cannot do</u>, based on the Word of God.
3. You must know <u>the truth</u> in the situation <u>and not just the facts;</u> based on the Word of God.
4. You must know <u>what you should or should not be saying</u>, based on the Word of God.
5. You must know <u>what you should or should not be doing</u>, based on the Word of God.

We have been conditioned to place credence in what, so-called credible, people say. We say what we hear them saying. For example, "The doctor said that I have this condition", or "My lawyer says this about my case", or "My mother, grandma or my pastor said the Bible says this or that". But if you want to have a strong confidence in your confession, you will have to find out what God's Word says for yourself. Then you will be able to have confidence in the one who cannot and will not ever lie. Then you can say with confidence and boldness that God said: "By Jesus' stripes I am healed" or "He will supply all my needs according to His riches in glory," when I sacrificially give to my man or woman of God for the work of God!

Growing up, my mother and I were poor. She was single, blind and very sickly and therefore had to be on "welfare". But my mother never let me go without the necessities of life and I always had great Christmases. How you may wonder? Evelyn was the queen of the lay-away!

The confession of our faith works along the lines of the lay-away plan. When you understand that you have already been blessed with every spiritual blessing in heavenly places and that God has already given you all things that pertain to life and godliness, then you will understand that the raw material for every one of your needs already exits in one of heaven's warehouses. When you ask God for what you want in faith believing that you have received it, the moment that you prayed, then an angel goes into the particular warehouse where your item is stored and he tags it. It is now on lay-away. The confession of the Word of God, or the confession of your receipt of the thing you are believing for, is equivalent to making your lay-away payments.

When you purchase something on lay-away, you walk away with the receipt, but you don't have it yet. Nevertheless you walk away telling everyone that you know what you have just bought; although you have no evidence of it other than you receipt. You even go home and start moving stuff around to make room for what is coming out of the lay-away. In that same light, when you have confidence in your confession, you go to work with what you have and start talking about it. You start saying it. You start acting just like you did when you made your last lay-away payment and they brought what you paid for to your house.

The Word of God is your receipt as it were. Faith, which comes from the Word of God, is the evidence or title-deed (according to the Amplified Version) of what you are believing and confessing that you have received. When you begin to confess God's Word and your faith begins to work to its fullest extent, then what you are believing for is released from heaven's warehouse into your life. Just keep on making those lay-away payments or confessing the Word over your situation

Assignments:

1. Familiarize yourself with the Faith Scriptures from this week's lessons.

2. Complete the study questions from week one.

3. Attend Church on Sunday and a Family Life Cell Group next week.

FAITH CONFESSION:

My angels are working for me right now to bring heaven's provisions.

1. Name the three components of the faith process that have been discussed in these last three lessons.

   _____

   _____

   _____

2. What is a faith confession?

   _____

   _____

   _____

3. The seed in the parable of the Sower in Matthew 13 and Mark 4 is synonymous with what?

   _____

4. The ground in this parable of the sower is synonymous with what?

   _____

5. In which two ways does the devil challenge the faith process in your life?

   _____

6. Please fill in the blank - Words are _____ of spirit and life.

7. Name three things that are affected in the spirit realm by the confession of your faith.

_____

_____

_____

8. A faith confession must be which of the following?

      A. Personal   B. Present Tense   C. Persistent

      D. None of the above   E.   All of the above

9. Confidence is based on _____.

10. Which five things do you need to know in order to have confidence in your confession?

_____

_____

_____

_____

Week No. 5
The Faith Regimen - Component 4: Doing

"But be doers of the Word and not hearers only, deceiving yourselves". **(James 1:22)**

CENTRAL THEME: The doer of the Word of God must add actions that line up with their confession.

ADDITIONAL VERSES: James 2:14-22 **(Amplified Version);**

All too often, believers make the mistake of confessing their faith in the Word of God while at the same time they contradict their confessions with wrong actions. They say that they are trusting God to provide for their financial needs, yet at the same time they won't do the things that the Word of God says will get the blessing on their finances. They rob God by not tithing or giving offerings. They also spend much of their time worrying about how they are going to pay bills or make their money stretch. There is no corresponding action there at all. You have to not only be an asker in line with the promises in the Word, or be a believer in the Word or a confessor of the Word of God; you have to be a doer of the Word of God. This means that your actions must correspond with your asking, believing and confessing, if you are to receive from God.

In the 2nd Chapter of James he states that when faith cooperates with our works, our faith is completed and reaches its supreme expression. Now the book of James was not written about salvation. The Apostle James was writing to Christians, for in verse 14 of James 2, he said, "What good is it **my brethren**, if a man confesses to have faith and yet his actions do not correspond?" James was writing to believers, pointing out that faith without works or corresponding actions will not work for them, even though they were Christians.

Our foundation verse says that we are to be doers of the Word and not just hearers of the Word, or else we become self-deceived. There are many self-deceived or self-deluded people who blame their problems on the devil, their parents, the school district, society, their husband or wife or some other person; when in reality they have deluded themselves by not doing the Word. The actions of a doer of the Word will always coincide with their confession of faith.

In Matthew 7, the Lord Jesus shows us how this self-deception works. These people hear the Word of God but never do it. Then when the storms of life come (and they come to everybody sooner or later) we see these people's spiritual air castles come crumbling down all around them. Then the first thing they say is, "God why did you let this happen to me". The fact is...the storms of life come to everyone. God didn't let it happen to them, they didn't do what it took to build their house on a good foundation by being a doer of the Word of God and not just a hearer or listener to the Word of God. Notice here that one person's house stood in that self-same storm. The same wind and rain came upon both houses. But the reason one was destroyed and the other was not is because the wise person was a doer of the Word and the foolish one wasn't. It isn't the storms of life that defeat us. If the storms were what would defeat us, then we would all be defeated. It's that we never decided to do or act in line with the Word of God that defeats us.

Many who believe in Christ and declare that they believe God's Word from Genesis to Revelations are still sick, poor, confused, bitter and living in self-pity. They are truly saved, yet they are still living defeated lives. Why, because their actions don't line up with what they believe. In the next lesson we will look at different positions that people who say they are believers in Christ take in relationship to faith. There is a difference between hearers of the Word, talkers about the Word and doers of the Word. The way to make God's Word your own is to act on it or be a doer of it. Just do what it says to do. "Trust in the Lord with all your heart and lean not to your own understanding", is what the Bible says. You cannot trust in the Lord without trusting in His Word. I have people in my church, even ministers, who don't trust God. How do I know they don't trust God? Because they don't do what the Word of God says to do? They don't tithe and give. They don't forgive offenses against them. They don't speak the Word over their lives. They don't witness, invite and bring people to church. They don't pray daily. They don't serve anywhere in the ministry. They don't even read and study the Bible daily. And they don't attend church consistently. But they will tell you that they trust God. No, they don't!

When you trust in the Word of God with all of your heart and are not leaning on your human reasoning, then you will stop looking for people to be your solution. Some misguided Christians think, well the Republicans are the solution to the problems in this country. Other equally misguided Christians believe that the Democrats are the solution to the problems in this nation. But the truth is, only God is your solution...your answer. When you are trusting in God's Word, then your actions will be in perfect agreement with your confession of faith.

Until there are corresponding actions to your confession, there will be continual failure in your faith walk. If you confess or say that God is the strength of your life, but at the same time you continue to think and talk about all of your weaknesses, then you will live a defeated life. Why, because there are no corresponding actions with your confession. We are told in the Scriptures that we are to think on things that are true, honest, just, pure, lovely of a good report, virtuous and praise-worthy. This is part of being a doer of the Word of God. Too many times people say, well the thing that I am thinking on is true. Maybe, but is it lovely...is it pure...is it a good report? The reason that God tells us to think on these things is so that the devil cannot defeat us through improper thinking. We will talk about this more in another lesson this week.

FAITH CONFESSION:

I am not only a hearer of God's Word; I am a doer of the Word.

"Examine yourselves, whether you are in the faith; prove your own selves..." **(2 Corinthians 13:5).**

CENTRAL TRUTH: You need to locate your position in faith by a thoughtful examination.

ADDITIONAL VERSES: James 2:26

The Scriptures say that "...as the body without the spirit is dead, so faith without works is dead also." In our foundational verse, we are told to examine ourselves to see if we are in faith. Why? Because before you and I can be successful in the faith development process, we must locate ourselves relative to our position or orientation regarding the operation of the God kind of faith. We will look at seven (7) positions that people in the body of Christ take in regards to faith:

1. Anti-Faith – Are you one of those in the body of Christ who are simply <u>against</u> faith and the teachers of faith. If you are, then you need to re-examine your position in the light of all that the Scriptures have to say about faith (and what I have taught you in this study guide).

Hebrews 11:6 (NKJV) [6]But without <u>faith</u> *it is* impossible to please *Him,* for he who comes to God must believe that He is, and *that* He is a rewarder of those who diligently seek Him.

James 1:4-8 (NKJV) [4]But let patience have *its* perfect work, that you may be perfect and complete, lacking nothing. [5]If any of you lacks wisdom, let him ask of God, who gives to all liberally and without reproach, and it will be given to him. [6]But let him ask in <u>faith</u>, with no doubting, for he who doubts is like a wave of the sea driven and tossed by the wind. [7]For let not that man suppose that he will receive anything from the Lord.

Mark 11:22 (NKJV) So Jesus answered and said to them, "Have <u>faith</u> in God.

2. Argumentative Faith – Are you one of those in the Body of Christ who continually argues about how faith should be released, but you rarely, if ever actually exercise faith to the end in order to receive the promise of God?

3. Academic Faith – Are you in the group of believers who search the Bible about faith, studying it night and day from the Hebrew and from the Greek, but still you never exercise faith to partake of the supernatural power of God that He has made available to you. You don't ask God for anything (especially anything big), you don't believe for anything, and/or you don't confess the promises of God as a present reality in your life.

4. Apathetic Faith – These are individuals who were not properly instructed in faith or who didn't have the spiritual resolve to see the faith process through and therefore failed in obtaining their desired results or didn't see results take place fast enough. They believe that faith works, but they no longer make the development of their faith a priority.

5. Articulators of Faith – This group talks a good talk about faith, but never does anything. They have no corresponding actions.

6. Admirers of Faith – These people simply love to watch and admire other people in the Body of Christ exercise faith. They say to themselves, "Man, isn't that something!" But they also are short on action. Are you in this group?

7. Activated Faith – Finally there are Christians who are willing to act on the Word of God. They are willing to step out and believe for his wisdom, favor, blessings, strength and His mighty, miraculous, miracle working power to be released in their situation! These are the people who work the faith process and actually obtain the promises of God.

FAITH CONFESSION:

I am a doer of God's Word and not just a talker about God's Word.

"...do not become lazy, but <u>imitate</u> those who through faith and patience inherit the promises.
(Hebrews 6:12)

CENTRAL TRUTH: Miracles usually come with an instruction.

ADDITIONAL VERSES: Ezekiel 36:26-30; Joshua 6:1-6; 2 Kings 4:1-7; Luke 6:17-19; 8:43-45; Cp. Also Mark 6:56; Mark 2:1-5

In the Old Testament we find many, many examples of the children of Israel that revealed their faith by their actions. Almost every miracle in the Old Testament was preceded by an instruction from God. Under the Old Testament, God's covenant people didn't have the Holy Spirit living inside of them. Only the Priests, Prophets, Potentates (Kings), and in the early days, the Judges had the Spirit of God or the anointing of God upon them. Faith is believing and acting on the Word of God. As we have said, this Word may be the written Word, or what we call the Logos Word of God. Or this Word may be the Word spoken by the Spirit of God, which we call the Rhema Word of God. Under the Old Covenant, this Rhema came primarily through the prophets to God's people. New Covenant prophets don't guide; they confirm.

In the sixth chapter of the book of Joshua, God gave Joshua instruction's regarding taking the city of Jericho. God said that the army was supposed to walk around Jericho once every day for six days. Then on the seventh day, they were supposed to walk around the city seven times that day. They were also instructed not to say anything the first 12 times that they walked around the city, then after the 13th time they were to shout with everything that was in them. As you know, the walls of Jericho fell down and the Israeli soldiers were able to go in and plunder the city.

In 2 Kings there was a widow who acted upon the instructions that she was given by God through the prophet Elisha. Her husband was in Elisha's school of prophets. He also faithfully served Elisha, doing everything that he could to insure the success of Elisha's ministry. However, for some unexplained reason, this lady's husband died leaving the family in severe debt. This debt was so severe that her creditors were going to sell her sons into slavery in order for this debt to be paid off. This widow came to Elisha, explaining the situation to him. Elisha then gave her a plan of action that she acted on and when she did, it produced a miracle for her and her sons financially.

In the New Testament, there was a woman in the Bible who had a severe condition that caused her menstruation to never end for several years. It was probably caused by fibroid tumors or something akin to that. At any rate this woman heard that, just by touching the hem of Jesus' garment, people were being healing! She began to say, I too will be healed if I can but touch His clothes. She then put some "**determined action**" with her believing and confessing.

This woman pressed her way through a large crowd of people without giving up, even though the crowd didn't make it easy on her to get to Jesus. Once she touched Jesus, the power of God went out of Him into her and she was healed. Jesus told her: "Daughter, thy faith has made you well". Now I am sure that this woman had asked God to heal her prior to this. Notice also that once she heard about Jesus and how people were being healed through His ministry, she believed what she heard, though she wasn't present to witness these things. Then she began to say or confess that if she touched His hem, she too would be healed. But it wasn't until she was a doer (or acted on what she believed) by adding "corresponding actions" to her asking, believing and confessing that her "faith" made her well. So faith requires all of these ingredients: asking, believing, confessing and doing or acting on what you ask, believe and confess.

Also in the book of Mark, we find the incident where four men brought their friend to Jesus so that He could heal him. However the house that Jesus was ministering in was so full, they couldn't get in. They had to cut a hole through the roof and ceiling, and then they let this man down in front of Jesus via a rope. This was another demonstration of bold, determined action. The Bible says that Jesus "saw" their faith. How did He see their faith? He saw their faith through their actions. Faith without works or corresponding actions is dead.

From these passages, and many others, we can see that in order to operate in the God kind of faith, you must have the discipline to obey either the Logos (the written Word of God) or the Rhema (the spoken Word of God). You must do specifically what God tells you to do.

FAITH CONFESSION:

My bold, determined actions of faith lead to me receiving from God.

"And all these blessings shall come upon you and overtake you, because you OBEY the voice of the Lord your God..."

CENTRAL THEME: Blessings follow obedience!

As a young Christian I was taught, "blessings follow obedience". My friend, Dr. William Martin, always says regarding receiving God's blessings: "The main ingredient is to be obedient". Obedience involves bold, determined actions that are consistent with your asking, believing, and confessing. Back on Day 8 (You may want to review that day) we told you that there are about six things that you can expect to come to pass as you walk through the faith process. These six manifestations are things that you must expect to occur, as you need them as you walk through the faith process. They are God's wisdom, God's favor, God's plan of action, sustenance, strength to endure and if necessary, miracles.

First of all, it is vital for you to maintain these "*provisional* expectations" if you are going to be successful in your faith process. For smaller things, you may not need all of these provisional expectations. However as you begin to stretch your faith to believe for larger faith projects, these expectations will be crucial for you to receive. Because many believers have not understood the importance of these short-term expectations they have given up on those large faith projects and never brought to completion their faith project. Your actions must be in agreement with these expectations. If you get wisdom and do not apply it, it does you no good. If you get a plan of action, and do not work the plan, it does you no good. If you get an instruction for a miracle (in other words, the Holy Spirit tells you to do a certain thing for your miracle to be activated) and you don't follow the instructions, your miracle will never occur. If God raises up somebody to help you and you don't accept the favor of God that He sends your way, it does you no good.

Back in 1981, the Lord directed me to attend Rhema Bible Training College in Broken Arrow, OK. I was very new to the faith walk, but I had been given a good foundation in faith. I received a letter from the Dean of the College instructing me to make sure that I had enough money to attend the school without worrying about my finances. It had been their experience that many students who attended failed to receive all that God had for them due to the fact that they were in over their heads financially. Well after considering my financial situation, I went to the Lord in prayer and asked Him to make up for that which I was lacking financially. Within several days my pastor brought a woman who formerly attended our church to me. This woman told me that God had directed her to pay my entire tuition to Rhema. Well I had been raised in such a way that my conscience would not allow me to accept this amount of money from someone who wasn't family. As I was about to tell her that I couldn't accept this, the Holy Spirit said to me: "Don't miss your blessing and don't make her miss her blessing". Her blessing was in giving, which set her up for God's financial blessings in a greater way in her life. We will address that later in this material. So I accepted it. This was several thousands of dollars. At the time I didn't know much about the favor of God, but thank God the wisdom of God that came to me from the Holy Spirit enabled me to accept the favor of God that He was directing my way. God will raise up somebody or some "some bodies" to help you but you must accept it.

FAITH CONFESSION:

I am obedient to the Word of God and the leadings of the Holy Spirit!

WEEK 5
The Regimen of Faith – Component 4: <u>D</u>oing
Day 33
Four Things Required to Consistently Operate in Obedience

"If you are willing and obedient, you will eat the good of the land." **(Isaiah 1:19)**

CENTRAL THEME: Ingredients involved in consistent obedience.

ADDITIONAL VERSES: John 5:44; 2 Corinthians 10:3-6; Mark 4:13 – 18; Hebrews 4:14

Our foundational verse for today tells us several things. First it informs us that God wants us to eat the good of the land. Second it tells us that you and I have to be willing. This is two-fold. We must be willing to eat the good of the land. God's not going to force good things on you. God's not going to make you take abundance, healing, peace, joy and victory...you must be willing. You can hear this kind of teaching and read this from the Word all you want but if your attitude is that it's just not for you, then God won't make you take it. The other part of being willing is that you have to be willing to do whatever God says that you must do in order to get it. Finally this verse reveals to us that to be obedient is also an essential ingredient to eating the good of the land. Today, I want to share four things that are required to keep you walking in obedience.

First, in order to consistently operate in obedience, you must be wiling to take bold, determined actions in agreement with the Word of God without always fully understanding everything. These actions must however, never compromise your integrity or witness as a Christian.

Second, in order to consistently operate in obedience, <u>the opinion of other people can no longer dominate your thinking</u>. God's acceptance must become the most important thing to you. If you need acceptance from anyone other than God, you will be tempted to compromise in your faith walk. Many times faith requires actions that your family, friends, associates and neighbors may not understand. So if you need the approval of others, you may not be able to act very boldly.

Third, in order to consistently operate in obedience, you must learn to govern your own thought life. The Scriptures teach us that we have to cast down imaginations and every thought that exalts itself against the knowledge of God. Failure, defeat, sickness & lack are all contrary to the knowledge of God's Word. If you sit around thinking about how this won't work, or won't work for you, then you are thinking contrary to the knowledge of God. You must purposefully cast these thoughts down, in the name of Jesus!

Finally, in order to consistently operate in obedience, you must utilize God's grace, in order to obey under extreme pressure. Once you step out in faith, you must see things to the end no matter how great the pressure gets (and I can assure you that there will be pressure to quit).

Jesus said in Mark 4 that whenever one receives the Word of God, the devil will come to steal that Word from your heart. He will either use tribulations (circumstantial pressure) or persecution ("the collective" pressure) to get you to let go of your grip on the Word and on faith. Collective pressure, or pressure from people who don't understand your faith stance is often the most difficult pressure. That's why the Bible says you must hold fast to your confession of faith. <u>Pressure is always going to come to get you to say uncle</u>. You must learn to resist the pressure and fight through the pressure. If you don't, you will always be starting and stopping in your faith walk. It doesn't matter what church you go to or how many Scriptures you can quote. The thing that separates the men from the boys and the women from the girls is your ability to maintain your dedicated determination to hold steady in faith through to the end. We will talk more about that next week when we talk about patience or enduring.

I know people who have been in faith churches for years, even graduated from Bible College, but they don't understand that they must fight through the pressure, so they never complete a faith project personally or in ministry. Then they become Anti-Faith, Academicians of Faith, Admirers of Faith or Articulators of Faith, but not Actors on Faith, so they dry up in their faith walk.

FAITH CONFESSION:

Because I am willing and obedient, I eat of the good of the land.

"If they obey and serve Him, they will spend their days in prosperity, and their years in pleasures". **(Job 36:11).**

CENTRAL THEME: Faith requires bold determined actions that correspond with your believing.

Today's foundation Scripture is one of the most powerful that I have ever read on the subject of obedience. Look at it: "If they (you and I) obey, they (you and I) will spend their (our) days in prosperity and their (our) years in pleasures. Obey today and have prosperity and pleasure tomorrow! That's what this verse is telling us. However, sometimes it is difficult for people to act with bold, determined actions. Why do faith actions or actions of obedience sometimes seem difficult? There are several reasons for this:

First, it is because bold determined actions cannot just be taught. They must be acted out. That's why it's important to stay around people of faith so you can see how they do it. Some things are better caught than taught.

Second, bold determined actions may put you at odds with those people that you seek acceptance from. Sometimes you'll try to discuss what bold actions you are going to take and these people will try to talk you out of it. I remember that just before I went to Bible College, when I was 20 years old, the Holy Spirit told me to purchase a car before I went. To make a long story short, I spoke with two individuals that I thought had a lot of wisdom, but in truth, I also needed their acceptance over my decision. I let them talk me out of it and ended up walking and riding a ten-speed bicycle almost the entire time that I was away attending Bible School.

Third, bold determined actions may push you outside of your ordinary limits or your comfort zone. However, once you begin to consistently operate outside of your comfort zone long enough, then that becomes your new comfort zone.

Fourth, bold determined actions may involve some short-term discomfort. However short-term discomfort will reveal the potential that is in you and cause you to grow through the discomfort.

Fifth, bold, determined actions may be required even when you are not fully persuaded on the promise of God yet. In order to take bold actions you must be fully persuaded.

Finally, it may be difficult for you to operate in bold, determined actions because of your personal ignorance of the faith process. That's why I have put together this Study Course, to help you overcome this area.

In 1980, God spoke to me in a voice from heaven saying, "Teach My people that they don't have to be sick, poor or ignorant". It is difficult to act in boldness if you are ignorant of the faith process. Now understand this, bold faith actions don't mean that you do something weird or strange. ***You can never force God to do something by taking outrageous actions.*** So you don't stop taking your medicine.

When I first started pastoring, I taught a series on divine healing. One of my newly saved men in my church heard that by Jesus' stripes we are healed; so he just stopped taking his medicine. He began to look and feel real bad. Then after two Sundays of teaching on healing I made a statement informing my congregation that because you believe that you are healed by Jesus' stripes that doesn't mean that you stop taking your medicine. Let your medicine address the physical symptoms, while your faith gets to the root cause of the sickness. Thank God I said that and he was there to hear it or other wise we could have had a disaster on our hands! And guess who would have been blamed for it: God and me (even though I had no knowledge that he had stopped taking his medicine)! Every since then I have been quick to inform or remind people that by not taking your medicine you don't automatically receive your healing. Medicine doesn't heal you. Medicine assists the natural healing processes that God placed in your body, or it assists certain systems in your body to function at a higher level. But medicine doesn't prevent the power of God from healing you. Medicine is not, in any way, contrary to the power of God. Just don't depend on the medicine without using faith in God's Word to receive total healing so that you no longer need the medicine to address the symptoms. Bold faith actions are actions in agreement with your faith. Bold action is going as far as integrity and wisdom will take you and no further.

FAITH CONFESSION:

Because I am a serve and obey God, I will spend my days in pleasure...

"For unto us was the gospel preached, as well as unto them: but the word preached did not profit them, not being mixed with faith in them that heard it". **(Hebrews 4:2)**

CENTRAL THEME: What corresponding actions actually entail.

ADDITIONAL VERSES: James 2:14-17; 2 Corinthians 10:3-6; Romans 4:19-20; Matthew 9:23

This week has been all about doing the Word or the critical nature of adding corresponding actions to our faith. Our foundational verse above refers to the children of Israel who died in the wilderness. God had given them clear-cut instructions to go into the Promised Land. They heard it, but they would not go in. The Word that they heard did not profit them because that didn't mix the Word with faith, or they did not add corresponding actions to faith by doing what God told them to do. In the area of corresponding action, it is imperative that you know and understand that you must mix the Word of God with faith. When the Bible instructs us to mix God's Word with faith, it is talking about doing or acting on the Word of God.

In the 2nd Chapter of the book of James, works there refers to corresponding actions in agreement with what you believe. It is important that you understand that you must be willing to take some bold, determined actions to go along with your faith. James also tells us that looking for results without corresponding actions is deception. He informs us that we can be victims of our own self-deception if we are hearing the Word and not acting on what we hear. If you think you are in faith and have no corresponding action, then you are deceiving yourself. Expectations of Bible results are only justified when we have corresponding actions to the Word of God. If you are in faith, you must operate in actions that are in agreement with your confession.

There are three areas that you must focus on if you are going to maintain your strong commitment to consistently and successfully operate in the area of corresponding actions. These are:

1. Corresponding <u>Thinking</u>;
2. Corresponding <u>Talking</u> &
3. Corresponding <u>Tasks</u>.

The first area involves the management of your thought life through <u>corresponding thinking</u>. Maintaining corresponding thoughts in agreement with what you are confessing is vital to your success. If you don't mange your thought life by keeping your thoughts in agreement with what you believe, you will let human reasoning and contradictory circumstances negate your faith.

When you begin declaring your faith and begin taking bold actions, the devil will come and oppose your words and actions with questions in order to plant doubt and unbelief in you so that you lose your resolve to hold fast to your confession of faith. In order to maintain corresponding thoughts, you must think in line with your confession and with what the Word of God tells you to do. Abraham was strong in faith because he learned how to manage his thought life. Even though Abraham was fully aware of his utter inability to impregnate Sarah or for Sarah to conceive, he focused his thoughts on the Word of God. This allowed him to continue to grow strong in faith as he praised or gave glory to God.

The second area that you must focus on <u>corresponding talking</u>, if you are going to maintain your righteous resolve to consistently and successfully operate in the area of corresponding actions is to talk only in agreement with what you believe. You must be clear that when you are speaking in agreement with what you believe, you are purposely calling those things that be not as though they were. This is how you know that you are not in denial. When you clearly understand what you are doing then the devil can't defeat you. You are choosing to release your faith by speaking the Word on purpose, knowing that the Words that you speak are spirit and they are life!

Finally, you must focus on the <u>corresponding tasks</u> that are critical to the faith process. Corresponding tasks are those things that you do in agreement with what you believe. Always remember:

- Your actions should never compromise your integrity or Christian witness. You must never use hook or crook methods to achieve your faith goals. You must never "con" people. You must never manipulate people. Manipulation is just a form of witchcraft.

- Your actions should respect the natural process for the acquisition of a particular thing. In other words, what would you do first, in the natural, to acquire the thing desired? For example, you can't get a job unless you fill out an application; and you can't fill out an application unless you go out looking for a job or get on the Internet and pull up the application. This is the natural order of acquiring a job. If you are believing for a house, you must go and look for the house. Whatever the natural process is, this is where you must start. You must start in the natural, expecting the supernatural intervention of God!

- Your actions must always be to the degree or level of your faith. The Bible says be it unto you according to your faith. For example, your dream car may be a Bentley (like mine), but you may not have Bentley faith yet. So you must make a decision...are you going to walk until you get your Bentley, or will you get the car that your faith can produce now and continue to develop your faith for the Bentley, by developing streams of income that will allow you to purchase and maintain a Bentley. If you do this, you will eventually get your Bentley, Mercedes, Porsche, Escalade or whatever your dream automobile is.

In the area of healing it is important to take your medicine. **I can't stress this enough!** It is much easier to believe and confess the Word of God without pain or your blood pressure being dangerously high, than it is with your physical symptoms raging. The medicine works on the symptoms, while your faith works on the sickness. So take your medicine and continue to believe and confess the Word of God over your body daily, if not more!

- Your actions should be with diligence and persistence. Just because someone says no, doesn't mean that they have the final word on the matter. You must know that someone else out there has your yes, and stay persistent until you get it.

- Your actions must be for the right reasons. James says that one reason that people don't receive is for improper motives. God gives us all things richly to enjoy. God answers our prayer so that our joy may be full, not so we can show off or keep up with the Joneses.

- Your actions should be modeled after the example of successful others. So you need to know "how" someone else used their faith to get what they have, then imitate the principles that they acted on. This is why testimonies are so important. Every first Sunday we have testimonies during our Communion Service. You may be in the process of believing for a house and you may have been turned down. Well I was too! But when you hear that I was turned down the first time that I applied for the house that my family and I live in today; yet we persisted till we got it. I know of a pastor that was turned down 6 times before he got the house he believed for. This kind of sharing helps you to stay encouraged and to continue in faith until you get the thing you're believing for.

ASSIGNMENTS:

1. **Familiarize yourself with the faith Scriptures in the lessons from this week.**

2. **Complete the study questions for this week.**

3. **Attend your cell group and church this week.**

FAITH CONFESSION:

Because I am a serve and obey God, I will spend my years in prosperity!

1. **What is a simple definition of faith?**

2. **Which of the following statements is characteristic of those with Academic Faith?**

    A. Those in the Body of Christ who are simply against faith.

    B. Those in the Body of Christ who continually argue about how faith should or should not be released, but rarely or never release any faith themselves.

    C. Those who continually search the Bible about faith. They study the Greek and Hebrew concerning faith, but never operate in it.

    D. Those who talk a good talk about faith, but never does anything with there faith.

    E. Those who simply sit back and admire other people's faith and say to themselves, "Man, isn't that something! But they are also short on action.

3. **Name the main characteristic of "Articulators of Faith".**

    _____

4. **Name the main characteristic of "Admirers of Faith".**

    _____

5. **Name the main characteristic of "Arguers of Faith".**

    _____

6. **Name the main characteristic of "Actors on Faith".**

    _____

7. **What is the Logos Word of God?** _____

8. **What is the Rhema Word of God?** _____

9. **Name the "interim" expectations associated with faith:**

    _____

    _____

10. Acting in agreement with what you believe is called what?

_____

_____

11. What four things are required to operate in consistent obedience?

_____

_____

_____

_____

12. What is the Bible referring to when it mentions work?

_____

_____

13. When you begin to declare your faith and begin to take bold action, the devil will come and counter those words and actions with questions for the purpose of planting doubt and unbelief to challenge your confessions.

☐ TRUE   ☐ FALSE

14. You can believe right even though you are not thinking right.

☐ TRUE   ☐ FALSE

15. Your actions should never compromise your integrity or your Christian witness.

☐ TRUE   ☐ FALSE

16. Your actions should respect the natural order of acquisition of a particular thing.

☐ TRUE   ☐ FALSE

17. Your actions should be with diligence and persistence.

☐ TRUE   ☐ FALSE

18. Your actions don't have to be for the right reasons or motives.

☐ TRUE   ☐ FALSE

19. Your actions should also be modeled after the testimonies of successful others.

☐ TRUE   ☐ FALSE

Week No. 6
The Faith Regimen - Component 5: Enduring

"That you do not become sluggish, but imitate those who through faith and patience inherit the promises". **(Hebrews 6:12)**

CENTRAL THEME: You must develop tenacity to see your faith endeavor through to its successful end.

ADDITIONAL VERSES: Luke 21:19 Amplified Version; Romans 2:7 Amplified Version; Romans 5:3-4 Amplified Version; 2 Thessalonians 1:4 Amplified Version

As we have said throughout this study guide on faith, faith is believing and acting on the Word of God. We have also said that faith allows us to tap into the supernatural power of God in order to change circumstances and conditions in line with the Word of God. For every promise of God, every principle of Scripture and every prophecy of the Spirit, there is a faith process to bring it to pass.

However faith has a twin or a partner in its efforts called patience. In the above foundational verse, we see that it takes both faith and patience to inherit the promises of God. Here we see that Abraham not only inherited the promises through faith, but he also employed patience with his faith to obtain the promise of God. Today we will see how the biblical subject called patience has been grossly misunderstood in the Body of Christ. When biblical patience is understood, then you will see that patience doesn't take away from faith by compromising our believing or confessing of the Word of God. Patience doesn't draw back from the faith fight; patience actually turns up the heat in the faith battle. Patience fortifies you for the fight of faith. Scriptural patience isn't an attitude that causes one to have a sit back and see spirit...patience persistently attacks the situation until faith brings to pass the promise, principle or prophesy.

The tone and tenor of patience in the Scriptures reveals that biblical patience, like faith, is an active force rather than a passive time of waiting. The Greek word for patience is markrothumia, which means patient endurance and longsuffering. It involves perseverance, fortitude and persistence! We must change our view of patience! In Luke chapter 21, in the Amplified Version patience is referred to as patient endurance. In Romans 2 out of the Amplified Version, the Bible calls it patient persistence. In Romans 5, out of the Amplified Version, we find that it refers to patience as unswerving endurance and fortitude.

You must have a paradigm shift in your thinking relative to patience if you are to be successful in bringing to completion your faith projects. Most Christian's view of patience is that patience just sits back and waits to see what's going to happen. That's not patience, that's doubt and unbelief. Patience says, "Let's make something happen, in Jesus' name!" You may have to change the route you are taking to make it happen, but you do not sit back and do nothing. In 2 Thessalonians, Chapter 1, it tells us that the Thessalonians were steadfast, with unflinching endurance and patience when facing persecution, distresses or pressure and afflictions or hard times, which allowed them to be firm in their faith and hold up under pressure. Bishop Ira Hilliard says, "Patience or endurance is the spiritual resolve that gives birth to the strength and the tenacity to continue operating in faith in the face of "give-up" opportunities." You could give up, but you don't. Instead you put on patient endurance and the force of persistence or perseverance, which enables you to have more tenacity than you had before. I'd like to think, that among my most admirable qualities, I have operated with a tenacity of spirit that just will not quit! Faith says, "I can not be defeated!" Patience or Endurance says, "And I will never quit!"

FAITH CONFESSION:

I cannot be defeated and with patience's help, I will never quit!

"That you do not become sluggish, but imitate those who through faith and patience inherit the promises." **(Hebrews 6:12)**

CENTRAL THEME: Patience is the power twin to faith.

ADDITIONAL VERSES: Hebrews 10:36; Luke 8:15; 1 Timothy 6:12;

So far we have seen that faith has a twin or a partner in its efforts called patience or endurance. Patience or endurance is the partner to faith or (asking, believing, confessing and doing God's Word). May times in Scripture, both faith and patience are mentioned in pairs. In our foundational verse in Hebrews, we see that we inherit or obtain the promises of God through both of these spiritual forces. The larger the faith project, the more important the force of patient endurance will become to stabilizing and strengthening your faith.

In Hebrews the 10th Chapter we see again that patience works along side of faith to receive the promises of God. The Lord Jesus said that the only way to bring forth fruit is with patience. The Apostle Paul told his son in the Lord, Timothy, to fight the good fight of faith. When in any fight, one of the most important things that you must have going in is a commitment to finish. I never boxed in a league, but I did a lot of fighting growing up as a kid and even some in High School. The difference between me and most guys that I ever fought, was that I was willing to die before I would quit, and I knew that they weren't.

When you're ever in a faith fight, you should put on patience like the second wind of a boxer. Muhammad Ali was a great example of a fighter that always reached deep inside of himself to find a second wind for those "championship" rounds. Patience is the spiritual force that gives you the resolve to finish what you've started. Through patience, you will be able to put forth an effort that doesn't quit until it has obtained the thing that it has set its faith on.

FAITH CONFESSION:

Through patience I control my mind, will and emotions in the face of discouragement.

But if we hope for that we see not, *then* do we with patience wait for *it.* **(Romans 8:25 KJV)**

CENTRAL THEME: The Faith Process isn't a get rich quick scheme...patience is required.

ADDITIONAL VERSES: Hebrews 11:1; 1 Timothy 6:12

We have consistently said to you that faith is believing and acting on the Word of God. In fact faith is asking, believing, confessing and doing the Word of God or having actions that correspond with what we have asked, believed and confessed for. One component that we haven't talked about in this study on faith is hope. Hope is a confident expectation of good. The Word of God builds both faith and hope into our lives. Hebrews 11 says that our faith gives substance to the things that we hope for. In other Words, hope actually comes before faith. Hope is like the architectural drawing of a building that one proposes to build. Hope is the picture, the dream, the vision of what you want God to do for you through faith. Faith is the raw spiritual material that creates or brings to pass what we hope for. In our foundational verse in Romans 8 we see that what ever the picture is that we are using to bring to pass, not only requires faith, it requires patience.

Patience gives you the strength you need to endure hardship until your manifestation (the thing you are believing for) comes to pass. In the fight of faith, which may not be easy, there may be some things you will have to overcome. You are not going into this fight blindly. You understand ahead of time that this is a real fight, which means the enemy is actually trying to hurt you in order to keep you from the thing that you are believing for. Your fight isn't with God...it's with the forces of darkness that seek to keep your delivery from the spirit realm from ever occurring. Faith is not magic. Those persons who have developed strong faith are the people who understand the difficulty of the fight and yet persevere until they obtain the promise of God with their faith. The devil will turn up the heat to try to discourage you because he wants to keep you from seeing your faith work. The devil knows that once your faith works for you one time, you will become a different person; you will no longer be the same ever again.

Patience is also an incubator of faith, giving it time to grow so it can prevail in the fight of faith. Patience gives you time to recognize and process those provisional expectations that we talked about in a previous lesson. When you have done everything that you know to do, you understand that this principle must be allowed to continue to work in your life. If you step back, it is only to step back to see if you have applied wisdom properly. Have you worked the plan of action that God gave you properly? This is how you use the time involved with patience properly to process the interim expectations.

FAITH CONFESSION:

I am fighting the good fight of faith and winning, Glory to God!

²⁶And He said, "The kingdom of God is as if a man should scatter seed on the ground, ²⁷and should sleep by night and rise by day, and the seed should sprout and grow, he himself does not know how. **Mark 4:26-27 (NKJV)**

CENTRAL THEME: Patience isn't passive waiting, is persistent believing and acting.

ADDITIONAL VERSES: Colossians 1:10-11; Titus 2:1-2; Genesis 18:4

In our last lesson we saw that patience has an impact on our faith by giving us strength to endure and acts as an incubator to allow our faith to develop even while we are believing God. Today we will talk about how patience works or serves us as it impacts both the spiritual and natural world around us.

Patience allows the spiritual forces to impact the natural. When you are making your faith confessions, demons are stopped and angels are being assigned and released to carry out their tasks. Angels have to impact things in the natural realm. You're not any less intense while being patient because you know that your angels are working on your behalf. You can't see anything working in the natural, but you are totally convinced that something is happening. Your expectation is still heightened because you have put on patience.

When a person says, "I have put on patience. I am just going to wait and see," I know that they don't understand patience. If they say, "I have put on patience and it's on now," then I know that the person understands patience. Patience is not taking the "wait and see" position, patience says faith and I will fight this thing out till we win together.

Patience is also necessary because of the respect we must have for the element to faith called time. There are time factors that govern our manifestations. God Himself doesn't work on the basis of time; He works in what is better called timing. That's why He is never late. But even God is limited to certain time factors.

First, we can understand that God can't always bring things to pass instantly in our lives because we haven't yet grown up enough to handle that for which we are believing for. But patience helps us in this way: Even as I am believing God and growing I don't have to stop releasing my faith. I continue to patiently endure and walk in persistence and perseverance until I reach the point that I am ready to run a fortune five hundred business or a mega ministry. And during the interim, I am continuing to invest in myself by sharping my tools and adding to my toolbox. This is where so many miss it, when it comes to business or ministry. They stop learning and growing, so their business or ministry stops growing. God has to grow you first before he can grow your business or ministry.

Then there are natural time factors that we must deal with, as patience strengthens and undergirds our faith while we wait for our manifestation. It takes 9 moths for a woman to have a baby. No matter how great your faith is, you are not going to get pregnant and deliver a baby in two days. This is a natural time factor that even God is limited to. Many times in Scripture, God would predict that someone would have a baby and say either by this time next year, or according to the time of life you will have this baby.

Finally, there are time factors that are governed by the will of others. When releasing your faith for material things, emotional things, and for relational matters, it is important that you understand that a person's will is involved and that it may slow up your manifestation from occurring. For example, you may be believing for someone to receive salvation. That person may then go out and act like a complete fool right after you began praying for them. But with faith and patient endurance you will not allow that to move you.

FAITH CONFESSION:

I am allowing patience to have its perfect work in my life!

³We can rejoice, too, when we run into problems and trials, for we know that they help us develop endurance. ⁴And endurance develops strength of character, and character strengthens our confident hope of salvation. **Romans 5:3-4 (NLT)**

CENTRAL THEME: Until you learn to add endurance to your fight, you're still immature in faith.

ADDITIONAL VERSES: Hebrews 4:3; Romans 3:4; Numbers 23:19; 2 Peter 1:3-4

Notice that here in Romans 5, out of the New Living Translation the Bible says that endurance develops strength of character. Therefore we see that the development of patience or endurance is part of the maturing process of the believer. As you learn to patiently rest on the promises of God, you will begin to be aware of your spiritual growth. In other words, when you arrive at a point where you don't panic every time you receive bad news, you know that strength of character or Christian maturity is occurring in your life. You should reach a point where you become settled in your spirit and disciplined in your mind and emotions to stay the course of faith until God's promise comes to pass in your life. I've learned to rest in the promise of God understanding that He is not only able, but He is willing to do everything that He promised in His Word.

Many Christians have never arrived at the point where they believe this way. They're still trying to check and see if this Word is true. The Word is true whether it works for you or not, because God said it is true. In the 3ʳᵈ Chapter of Romans, the Bible says let God be true and every man be a liar. The Word of God is not true because it works for you; it is true because it is God's Word and He is not a liar! You have to settle this in your heart and mind. Without that kind of resolve, you will be quick to blame God for your failure to receive the promises of God. However there is a process in the development of your faith, where you may not be doing it right. But, if you are already totally persuaded that this is the Word of God even if it does not work for me, then you will quickly admit that it must be you who is doing something wrong; not God. Dr. Kenneth E. Hagin once wrote a little mini-book called "Don't Blame God".

In 2 Peter, we find a list of things that are necessary for the maturing of the saints. Patience is a part of this list. Even in life, you know your child is maturing when they quit crying over every little thing that happens to them. When they start enduring some things, you know they are growing. Sometimes people reach adulthood and never learn what I am sharing with you now. They grumble, murmur and complain when things don't go their way. I see pastors, pastor's wives, assistant ministers, deacons and leaders in the church cry over even simple things. It's time for us to grow up and learn to endure hardships as a good soldier, knowing that patience along with faith will see us through to victory! Stop crying and complaining...

FAITH CONFESSION:

I am growing in character as I grow in patience.

³For you know that when your faith is tested, your endurance has a chance to grow. ⁴So let it grow, for when your endurance is fully developed, you will be perfect and complete, needing nothing.
James 1:3-4 (NLT)

CENTRAL THEME: Others have secured faith's promised results through enduring and so can you!

ADDITIONAL VERSES: Psalm 139:23-24; Romans 4:17; Proverbs 27:17; Isaiah 57:19; Hebrews 13:15; Psalms 22:3; 2 Corinthians 5:17-19; Ephesians 2:8-10

Endurance is a spiritual force that is never idle. Challenges often occur with new things that require an element of patient resolve or patient endurance so we may get the full enjoyment from the product. For example, when we purchased our home, there were things that we had to get our builder to come back and correct, but we didn't decide to move just because everything wasn't perfect. No we let patience have its perfect work and worked through those problems.

You have not put on patient endurance if you are not willing to continue to believe, confess and do the Word of God. James 1:3-4 in the King James Version tells us that patience must have its perfect work. So patience is working something. Patience primarily causes something to happen inside of me, while faith causes things to happen around me. When a coach is patient with a player in sports, they continue to work with that player because they are saying that this player is going to get it or the player is going to get there. However if this coach puts the player off the team, the coach has lost patience with that player. They refuse to continue to work with that player. Patience works with us and on us. Patience must have its perfect or complete work on us and in us.

Patience's work allows you to do several things while you believe for your manifestation. Patience's work allows you to check up on your lifestyle. Is there something in my life that I'm not doing right? Psalms 139 says, "Search me O Lord". Ask Him to do so and He will!

Patience's work allows you to review the promise for which you're in faith for. Is this the promise you should be relying on? Is this a promise that God has made to you? In the Bible there are three kinds of promises:

1. *Prophetic* Promises, which are based on the prophetic time clock of God.

2. *Particular* Promises, which are those that God makes to a particular person or group of people.

3. *Predicated* Promises, which are promises that God gives to us that, are predicated upon us meeting certain condition. All of the predicated promises have a principle that must be met before the promise can be fulfilled.

Patience's work allows you to review your confession of faith. Romans Chapter 4 tells us that God calls those things that are not as though they were. We are to exercise the God kind of faith and call those things that be not as though they were also. Is your confession really according to the Word of God? Many people are making good positive statements, but they are not making faith statements. A positive statement is only a faith statement when that positive statement agrees with what the Word of God says. "I feel better" is not a statement of faith. It's a good statement, but the Bible doesn't say, "Thou shall feel better". The Bible says, "By his stripes ye were healed". A faith statement or confession has to agree with the Word of God.

Patience's work allows you to check up on your fellowship. Iron sharpens iron. Are the people around you supporting you or working against you? The Bible tells us not to be yoked up with unbelievers. During the time that patience is having its perfect work on you, check out the folks that are around you. Sometimes you will have to repair fellowship with people and other times you will have to disconnect from people

Patience's work allows you to manage your thought life. This gives you the opportunity to get your thoughts in order.

Patience's work allows you to check out your commitment to the principle of praise. In Isaiah chapter 57, the Bible says that God creates the fruit of our lips. That doesn't make sense if you don't know what Hebrews 13 says. It says that the fruit of our lips is the sacrifice of praise. You can get so involved in your corresponding action that you stop depending on God and depending only on your confessions and corresponding actions. Praise gets God Himself involved according to Psalms 22.

Patience's work allows you to check up on your commitment to the work of God. I've seen people get so caught up in their corresponding actions that they slack off of their work in the Kingdom of God. We are called to win the lost and to make disciples! Some people become so consumed with trying to have something, that they get totally in the flesh and abandon all of their spiritual commitments. The Bible says that you have been put here to do good works. So don't let anything interfere with the good work you are supposed to be doing.

FAITH CONFESSION:

Though my faith may be being tested, my endurance is growing.

"And so, after he had patiently endured, the obtained the promise". **(Hebrews 6:15)**

CENTRAL THEME: You must follow the examples of those who endured and obtained the promise of God.

ADDITIONAL VERSESE: 1 Kings 18:41-45; 2 Chronicles 7:1-14

The testimonies of victorious saints validate the partnership between faith and patience or endurance. Abraham is one of those victorious believers who demonstrated each component of the faith process that we have been discussing in this book. The sixth chapter of Hebrews tells us that Abraham obtained the promise after he patiently waited for 25 years by not staggering at the promise of God through unbelief. How long are you willing to wait? Patience strengthens you in the face of disappointment.

In 1 Kings, we see that Elijah prayed for rain. He had to put on endurance several times before there was any sign that his prayer was working. Elijah went up to the top of Mount Carmel and threw himself down on the ground and put his face between his knees. This was his posture for praying intensely. Even though he knew that God had already promised the answer, he still had to pray with fervency and persistency. Therefore we can say that there is intensity when you are in faith. Elijah was in faith because he asked, believed, confessed, and did some things (or manifested corresponding actions) based on what God had said to him. But it still required patient endurance and persistence in his believing to get results.

God had shut up heaven and there was no rain because of the people's sins or disobedience. They had gotten themselves into idolatry and all types of sexual immorality. They were no longer operating as a fair and just society. They had thrown out both God's statutes and judgments. But, after Elijah called the nation back to God through repentance, Elijah had the right to pray for rain because the Bible says that God would cause rain to return whenever the people repented. Then Elijah also had direct revelation from God. As a man of faith, Elijah was able to hear what nobody else heard. He heard abundance with the ear of faith before he could actually hear it with his natural ears or see it with his natural eyes. So Elijah sent some of his disciples to the sea and they came back saying that they saw nothing. But Elijah would not give up. Seven times in total Elijah sent them to the sea to check. Because Elijah put on patience, he wasn't about to give up or quit until he got the results that God had promised him, both in the Word of God and by His Spirit! No matter how small the results were, Elijah moved in faith. He then sent some of his followers to King Ahab to tell him to get off of the mountain before the rain would come and trap him on the mountain. There was no rain at the time. But, King Ahab had the good sense to listen to the prophet. Then the deluge of rain came, thus ending the 3 ½ years of drought and the subsequent famine.

ASSIGNMENTS:

1. **Familiarize yourself with the promises of God and faith Scriptures in this Section.**

2. **Complete the Study Questions for this Section.**

3. **Attend Church and your Family Life Cell Group this week.**

FAITH CONFESSION:
I follow the examples of faith and patience of those who
Have persisted until they obtained the promise!

1. Living by faith is a life lived by the principles of God's Word and not by feelings.

   ☐ YES   ☐ NO

2. What four things are required to walk in any spiritual truth?

   _____

   _____

   _____

   _____

3. Does the Will of God automatically come to pass?

   ☐ YES   ☐ NO

4. Name the five categories of promises in the Bible that we mentioned this week:

   A. _____

   B. _____

   C. _____

   D. _____

   E. _____

5. Name the variables of faith that effect manifestations of promises.

A. _____

B. _____

C. _____

D. _____

E. _____

F. _____

G. _____

6. Name the 15 steps of releasing your faith for healing.

A. _____

B. _____

C. _____

D. _____

E. _____

F. _____

G. _____

H. _____

I. _____

J. _____

K. _____

L. _____

M. _____

N. _____

O. _____

7. Name the 15 steps of releasing your faith for a material promise in the Word.

A. _____

B. _____

C. _____

D. _____

E. _____

F. _____

G. _____

H. _____

I. _____

J. _____

K. _____

L. _____

M. _____

N. _____

O. _____

Week No. 7
The Faith Regimen - Results: Fulfillment!

Such things were written in the Scriptures long ago to teach us. And the Scriptures give us hope and encouragement as we wait patiently for God's promises to be <u>fulfilled</u>. **Romans 15:4 (NLT)**

CENTRAL THEME: The end of the faith process is the fulfillment of God's promises in your life.

ADDITIONAL SCRIPTURELLS: 2 Corinthians 5:7; Romans 4:19-20; Galatians 3:13-14; Acts 10:34

For every promise, principle and prophecy, there is a faith process to bring it to pass! The Scriptures are filled with promises that God has made to His covenant people, which are to be obtained by faith. In this lesson we will take a more detailed look at how to release faith for the various promises of God.

II Corinthians says that we believers are to walk by faith and not by sight. Therefore faith is more than something that we do when we are in trouble...faith is a lifestyle! Living by faith is a life lived by the principles of God's Word and not by our feelings. Therefore, you must never judge the faith process by your feelings. How you feel is not a factor. The late Reverend Smiths Wigglesworth was fond of saying, "I'm not moved by what I feel or see. I am only moved by what I believe; and I believe the Word of God!"

The Bible says that Abraham did not consider his body or the deadness of Sarah's womb. Therefore you have to "not consider" how you feel. My greatest faith victories have come when my feelings were sending contrary signals. Feelings have nothing in the world to do with God's Word. You have to believe based on the Word of God and not whether or not you feel good about it.

The Scriptures are filled with the promise of God that He has made to His covenant people. Galatians 3 shows a universal principle that these promises must be obtained by faith. There is an answer to the question, "Why does it look like God is working for some and not working for others." The answer is right here. The promises of God are received by faith. God is no respecter of persons, or He doesn't show partiality. But God is a respecter of faith. If you want to receive the promises of God, then you must begin developing your faith until it reaches its peak level. Bro. Kenneth E. Hagin once said, "I can believe God today for one million dollars just as easily as I believed God for $100.00 dollars when I first started learning these principles of faith". Then he was quick to add that it took all of the faith that he had to believe in $100.00 in the beginning of his faith walk. By this time, it also took him all the faith he had to believe in the one time, one million dollar offering. I know of two occasions when Brother Hagin believed in a one time, one million dollar offering from one individual. He also believed in, at least on one occasion, a one-time two million dollar offering from one individual. He began to say: "There's coming a day when someone will write out a check to Rhema or Kenneth Hagin Ministries an offering check for one million dollars." It took about three years the first time and less time the second time, but it came in. Then he elevated his believing to two million dollars.

Reaching the point of peak potential, or your summit of faith, starts first with being exposed to proper instruction on the subject of faith. After being exposed to instruction, then you have to take it upon yourself to study. That means that you have to intensely look at it. Then, of course, you need a pattern and some examples of faith to follow. Paul told his disciples to follow him as he followed Christ. Finally, you must begin to practice the faith regimen laid out in this book. You must actually come out of the classroom of faith into the crucible of life and actually do it. You can never drive a car just by reading the DMV rulebook or by having someone explain the process to you. You have to get in the car, buckle your seat belt and merge into traffic at some point and begin driving.

FAITH CONFESSION:

As I read, believe and confess God's Word, my faith grows.

"Your iniquities have turned away these things, and your sins have withheld good things from you." **(Jeremiah 5:25).**

CENTRAL THEME: Faith is not magic, so there are variables that affect your faith manifestation.

ADDITIONAL VERSES: Deuteronomy 28:1-68; Acts 8:21; 2 Corinthians 9:6-9; Malachi 3:6-12; Romans 15:22; 1 Thessalonians 2:18; John 10:10; Mark 4; 15-19

There are variables that impact or effect the manifestation of the faith process. In our foundational Scripture for today, we find that our sins and iniquities can cause good things to be held back from us, even though we complete the faith process, as described in this book. I want to lay out for you several factors that impact on the faith process.

As you can see from above, the first variable that effects the fulfillment of God's promises in our lives is sin. Sin disavows the benefits of the righteousness that have been imputed or credited to our account through faith in Jesus Christ. Of the 68 verses in Deuteronomy 28, the first 14 verses talk about what happens if you obey and the last 54 of the verses talk about what happens if you disobey. I think God is trying to get across to us that we are not going to have His best if we live a lifestyle of sin and disobedience. You have two choices. You can have what the flesh will produce or you can have God's best by obedience to Him.

The second variable of faith is the will of man. God will not violate the human will. A person trying to believe for a husband or a wife may pick out somebody that they want to believe for, but God is not going to go against that person's will. Years ago, a young lady and her mother did just this where I was concerned. They told me that they had claimed me by faith and that there was nothing I could do about it, because they had believed that they had received. Thank God that that wasn't and isn't so! God will not go against that person's will. You may be praying for somebody who is trying to overcome sickness and disease. That person's will is also involved and you cannot override that person's will. The human will is the most dominant factor in the earth. One man's will, Adam, caused all the mess that we're in because of an act of his will. God will not override a person's will and Satan cannot override a person's will. Satan has to deceive you into making bad choices, but he can't make you do anything.

Another variable is the Word of God itself. You may ask why the Word of God would be a variable. It is a variable because God will not do anything that is inconsistent with the Word of God. You can't make God do something. Faith comes by hearing and hearing by the Word of God. Therefore the operation of faith is limited to what the Word of God says God will or will not do. God has limited Himself to operate only in a manner that is consistent with His Word.

The fourth variable is heart motives. Your results will be determined by the condition of your heart. If your heart is not right, it can affect the time factor. The parable of the sower is found in

Mark, Chapter 4. There the Bible says that "the earth" brings forth fruit of itself. In a natural situation, you can take quality seeds and sow them in different types of soil and the results will vary. The results vary not just because of the seed, but also because of the soil. The earth here is analogous of the heart or spirit of man. So, the quality or condition of your spirit is going to affect the faith process. If your heart is not right, your faith is not going to work right. You can do everything right (the asking, believing, confessing and corresponding actions) but if your heart is not right it will not work. In Acts chapter 8, the Apostle Peter showed us the importance of the heart being right when he told Simon the Sorcerer: "You have neither part nor portion in this matter, <u>for your heart is not right in the sight of God</u>." Your heart motive has to be right!

Another very important variable that is often misunderstood and therefore overlooked is "stewardship". When you and I are in faith, one of our expectations is favor and tithing and giving are spiritual principles that impact favor. The Bible says in 2 Corinthians, Chapter 9 that when we give, over and above the tithe, God will cause all favor to abound toward you and me. Well, If we are not first tithers and then givers, we don't' have access to God's favor. If we are not Firstfruit Givers and Tithers, Malachi, Chapter 3 says that we are living under the curse and the curse cancels the blessing.

The sixth variable is the natural order of things. God respects the order that He has set up. If you are believing God for a child, it takes nine months for a child to be born. You can't believe for a baby and give birth to a baby tomorrow. You can believe that you are going to conceive and deliver in 9 moths. That is the order that God has set up in the natural for conception and delivery and He has not and will not ever override that.

The last variable that we will look at is satanic hindrances. These are spiritual attacks of the enemy into your life to frustrate the faith process. The Bible says that the thief comes to steal from us. One thing that the Bible reveals is that the devil comes to steal the Word of God from us through persecution, pressures, problems, the lure of wealth and life's worries.

FAITH CONFESSION:

All the Blessings of Deuteronomy 28:1-14 are coming on me now.

"He sent His Word and it healed them." **Psalm 107:20 (Fenton Translation)**

CENTRAL THEME: The systematic steps involved in receiving healing by faith in God's Word.

In today's lesson we will begin looking at in a comprehensive way the steps that are involved in standing on the promises of God in the area of health and healing. Over the next two days, I want to look at about 15 steps that, when taken out of a believing heart with the right heart motive, will produce fulfillment in the area of healing.

1. You must know that healing is the will of God for you (Matthew 8:1-8). It is God's will to heal you.

2. Find the Scripture verses that promise you healing. There are many passages and stories in the Bible where Jesus either healed, or the Bible reveals that healing is part of His redemptive work, just as much as the forgiveness of sins (Psalms 103:1-3; Exodus 15:26; Matthew 8:17; 1 Peter 2:24).

3. Ask God for His healing power to be released into your body, based upon the promises for healing that you found in the Scriptures. Remember that 1 John 5:14 says that this is the confidence that we have in Him that if we ask anything according to His will He hears us. No matter how you feel, you must chose to believe the Word of God that says He has heard you when you prayed.

4. Write the Scriptures down and read them aloud, then meditate on how you would look and feel when your healing is manifested. (Habakkuk 2:2-4)

5. Fashion and speak a confession of faith that is in agreement with the verses that you have found. Remember that a faith confession is a statement that you make in agreement with the Word of God. You are choosing as an act of your will to say what God has said about you in His Word. 1 Peter 2:24 says that by (Jesus') stripes you are healed. So that is what you are going to say. If you say that you feel better when you don't then that is a lie. But this is not feeling; it is faith, so we don't say anything about our feelings. Besides, that's not what God's Word says. God says that by His stripes you were healed. So choose to make a statement in agreement with the Word of God.

6. Explore what can be done in the natural to bring the healing to manifestation. The Bible says that the natural is first. So, that means that you will go to the doctor. The doctor is going to work on the symptoms while you work on the sickness itself with your faith. Therefore, going to the doctor does not get you out of faith. That also means checking into proper nutrition and exercise.

7. Thank God daily for your healing, as a sacrifice of praise. God creates the fruit of our lips. So, in the midst of your pain and discomfort, you are going to thank God for your healing. You must continue to say, "Father God, I believe that I am healed by Jesus' stripes...so I thank you that I am healed, in Jesus' name." Continue to take your medicine and offer to God the sacrifice of praise because He creates the fruit of your lips, which is the sacrifice of praise. You are doing what you need to do in the natural by going to the doctor and following the doctor's instructions. You are also doing what you need to do by utilizing proper nutrition and exercise to improve your physical condition. Then you are doing what you need to do in the spiritual realm. You have the natural doctor working on you, but you also have the Spiritual Doctor (who has never lost a case) working on you.

8. Keep your thoughts consistent with the Word of God. Reject any thought that comes into your mind that is contrary to God's Word. Believing is up to you. You set the criteria for what you will believe. You choose to believe what God's Word says. The doctor gives you the facts in the natural, but you know what the truth is. John 17:17 tells us that God's Word is truth. The truth is that you are healed, even though the facts say you're not, because God's Word says that you are.

9. Listen to teaching tapes or C D's daily on God's Will to heal. Remember that Proverbs 4:20-22 says that if you put God's Word into your heart, that it will be medicine to all of your flesh. You don't need to or have time to listen to Jazz, Hip-hop, Classical, R&B, Country and Western, or anything else for that matter, while you are driving in your car. You are working on something. You need to be working on receiving your healing. Therefore you should be listening to the Word. Take your natural medicine, but also take your spiritual medicine.

10. Avoid debates with those who don't believe. You don't have time to be involved or even around folks that don't believe. The Bible says in Mark 5:35-42, that Jesus went to heal Jairus' daughter. The girl was dead and the people were crying, but Jesus said she was asleep. The people stopped crying and began to laugh at Jesus. Jesus put them all out of the house. He didn't even keep unbelievers in His presence when it came to a faith fight.

There are some people you don't need around you when you are in a fight, especially if it is a terminal situation. There are some people who have seen sickness and disease win so many times that they have no faith in their hearts to believe you can be healed. Some folks have not seen enough victory in the area of healing. Therefore, in the tough times, they cannot stand with you.

FAITH CONFESSION:

God is my Great Physician.

"He sent His Word and it healed them." **Psalm 107:20 (Fenton Translation)**

CENTRAL THEME: Systematic steps involved in receiving healing by faith in God's Word.

In today's lesson we will finish looking at the steps that are involved in standing on the promises of God in the area of health and healing. Yesterday we got as far as step 10. Today we will begin with step 11 and go to step 15.

11. Follow the doctor's orders. Following the doctor's instructions will not affect your faith. Don't get intimidated and allow the devil to push you into not doing what the doctor tells you to do. Just like he tempted Jesus in Mark 4:1-5, the devil will say to you, if you really believe you are healed, you should not take medicine. Many people die like that. They wait too late. If you are in a relay race and the person that you are racing with gives you the baton late and the runner that you are running against has a 50-yard jump on you, you can't catch up unless someone slows him down or trips him. In this sense, if you get the baton late, the doctor can slow the symptoms down enough for your faith to catch up. Just because you got the baton late does not mean you are going to lose, if you will allow the doctors and medicine to work on the sickness to slow it down.

12. Get with others who understand the faith process and have them to agree with you for your healing. You don't need sympathy. Matthew 18:18-19 says that if any two shall agree on earth as touching anything it shall be done of the Father God. You need someone who understands the faith process to stand with you, support you and believe God with you for your healing.

13. Don't panic if the healing doesn't manifest instantly. Many times healings that are received by faith take place progressively. There are cases in the Bible where it says that from that point in time where the person believed, they began to amend. In Mark 16:18, the Bible says that the sick would recover. Recovery indicates a progressive occurrence, not necessarily an instant one. Don't confuse miraculous with instantaneous. Anything that God does is a miracle. The miracle may simply take place over time. There is something in the Word of God known as gifts of healings and the workings of miracles. When they are in operation, healings usually occur instantly. However, here we are not talking about receiving your healing through spiritual gifts,

we are talking about receiving your healing by faith. So you are not going to let your self get frustrated if when you pray or are prayed for and your healing is progressive.

14. List the symptoms and rejoice as each symptom disappears. When you start off in this fight, you should list all of the symptoms – pain, headache, limitations on the use of a body part, fever, etc. List them all because you are going to chart their disappearance. At one time you may not have been able to move your arm very well or at all. But now, after prayer, you might be able to wiggle your fingers. Rejoice in all of the small victories, just as if the entire process was complete. First that shows gratitude. Second it will boost your faith and remind you that *the process* is working.

15. Maintain an attitude of joy all through the process. This is the strengthener of your faith. The Bible says that the joy of the Lord is our strength. In Proverbs 17:22, in the Amplified Bible, we are also told that a joyful attitude of faith and a merry heart does good like a medicine. Your attitude and your mindset will help the process. So, you are not looking for everybody to feel sorry for you. Some people don't want to get healed because they will have to start doing things for themselves.

FAITH CONFESSION:

I am healed from the top of my head to the souls of my feet.

"What things that you desire, when you pray, believe that you receive them and you will have them"
(Mark 11:24).

CENTRAL THEME: Systematic steps involved in receiving material things by faith in God's Word.

In today's lesson we will begin taking a comprehensive look at the steps that are involved in standing on the promises of God in the area of material and financial matters. We will look at about half of the 15 steps that, when taken out of a believing heart with the right heart motive, will produce fulfillment in the area of material prosperity.

1. You must know that it is God's will to bless you with material things. God gives us all things richly to enjoy (1 Timothy 6:17).

2. Find the Scripture verses that promise you material blessing. There are many passages and stories in the Bible that promise us prosperity and material blessings. (Cp. Deuteronomy 8:18; Proverbs 37:25; Mark 11:24; 2 Corinthians 8:9; Philippians 4:19)

3. Ask God for the thing that you want in line with the promise you found in the Scriptures. Remember that 1 John 5:14 says that this is the confidence that we have in Him that if we ask anything according to His will He hears us. No matter how you feel, you must chose to believe the Word of God that says He has heard you when you prayed.

4. Write the Scriptures down and read them aloud, then meditate on how you would look and feel with the thing that you are believing for.

5. Fashion and speak a confession of faith that is in agreement with the verses that you have found. Remember that a faith confession is a statement that you make in agreement with the Word of God. You are choosing as an act of your will to say what God has said about you in His Word. Mark 11:23 says: "What things you desire when you pray, believe that you receive them and you shall have them". God says that you would receive, so you will receive. So choose to make a statement in agreement with the Word of God.

6. Explore what can be done in the natural to acquire the thing. Can you work some overtime? If there is no overtime available, believe God for it. Can you take on a part time job?

7. Thank God daily for the thing that you believed you have received as a sacrifice of praise (Hebrews 13:17; Isaiah 57:19).

8. Sow a financial seed for God's grace, which includes His wisdom and favor for the acquisition of the thing. You have to give. When Abraham wanted some wisdom on how to obtain his inheritance, GOD TOLD HIM TO GIVE HIM AN OFFERING (Genesis 15:1-8)! Supernatural things happen when we give. Sow a seed for God's grace (2 Corinthians 9:6-9) to be released in your life. The Bible also says that you can make a vow and after you pay your vows, you can decree a thing and it shall be established and the light of God's favor will shine on you (Job 22:27-28)! Please obtain my books entitled: "FIRSTFRUITS: God's Plan to Propel you from Poverty to Prosperity" and "God's River of Prosperity" for more insight on this subject.

FAITH CONFESSION:

Money Cometh to me in abundance, right now, in Jesus' name!

"What things that you desire, when you pray, believe that you receive them and you will have them"
(Mark 11:24).

CENTRAL THEME: Systematic steps involved in receiving material things by faith in God's Word.

In today's lesson we will finish our comprehensive look at the steps that are involved in standing on the promises of God in the area of material and financial matters. We will look at the remainder of 15 steps that, when taken out of a believing heart with the right heart motive, will produce fulfillment in the area of material prosperity.

9. Keep your thoughts consistent with the Word of God. Reject any thought that comes into your mind that is contrary to God's Word. Believing is up to you. You set the criteria for what you will believe. You choose to believe what God's Word says.

10. Listen to teaching tapes or C D's daily on God's will to prosper you. Remember that Proverbs 4:22 says that out of your heart flows the issues or literally, the boundaries of life. Faith comes by hearing and hearing by the Word of God (Romans 10:17).

11. Continually confess that you have the wisdom of God and that God orders your steps.

12. Avoid debates with those who don't believe. Don't debate with them. Just tell them to hide and watch (Titus 3:9).

13. Find a mentor who used their faith as an example and learn from them and their successful efforts. Find somebody who used their faith to get a certain object and find out how they did it (Cp. Hebrews 6:12).

14. Diligently follow the natural order to the full extent of your integrity. In other words, diligently do everything you can do without compromising your integrity or Christian witness. Don't try to drop hints to people who can help you. That is manipulation. I know women who have a man for fixing their car, another for paying their utilities and another for cash money. That is not faith.

There's a Word for it, but it's not faith. Then there are guys who use women in much the same way. Stop it.

15. Don't get frustrated in the process; remember that just as with healing, the results are progressive. Maintain an attitude of joy all through the process, charting your progress and rejoicing at each step you make towards your goal.

FAITH CONFESSION:

All my needs are met according to God's riches in glory...!

"What things that you desire, when you pray, believe that you receive them and you will have them" **(Mark 11:24).**

Well congratulations child of God, you have completed 50 days of the study of faith! These are time tested and proven principles that will not only help you gain an intellectual understanding of the subject of faith, but that will enable you to come out of the laboratory of faith and onto the launch-pad of faith so that you may apply them to your daily life.

For every promise of Scripture, every prophecy of the Spirit and every principle of the kingdom, there is a faith process that is necessary to bring it to pass. Faith is basically believing and acting on the Word of God. Faith involves five specific components:

(1)   Asking
(2)   Believing
(3)   Confessing
(4)   Doing &
(5)   Enduring

When these five components are operated in a disciplined regiment, out of a properly motivated heart, together they will result in a sixth thing: Fulfillment (or success)! The Scriptures declare emphatically that your faith is the victory that overcomes the world and that your faith will allow you to live at the highest level of life possible. I want to thank you for participating in this Spiritual Growth Campaign for the last 50 days. I also want to encourage you to read the entire book over as often as you need and to and to refer back to particular subjects as you embark on the greatest adventure in life, the adventure of faith.

If you participated in this 50 Day Spiritual Growth Campaign, and don't have church home and you live in the Southern California area, I would like to extend an invitation to you to worship with us this Sunday. Just go to www.calvarfi.com for directions and more information.

FAITH CONFESSION:
By faith I too hear the sound of abundance for my life!

---

1. Living by faith is a life lived by the principles of God's Word and not by feelings.

   ☐ YES   ☐ NO

2. What four things are required to walk in any spiritual truth?

   _____

   _____

   _____

   _____

3. Does the will of God automatically come to pass?

   ☐ YES   ☐ NO

4. There are five categories of promises in the Bible. What are they?

   A._____

   B._____

   C._____

   D._____

   E._____

5. Name the variables of faith that effect manifestation of promises.

   A._____

   B._____

   C._____

   D._____

   E._____

   F._____

   G._____

6. Name the 15 steps of releasing your faith for healing.

A._____
_____

B._____
_____

C._____
_____

D._____
_____

E._____
_____

F._____
_____

G._____
_____

H._____
_____

I._____
_____

J._____
_____

K._____

L._____
_____

M._____
_____

N._____
_____

O._____
_____

7. Name the 15 steps for releasing faith for a material promise in the Word of God.

A._____

_____

B._____

_____

C._____

_____

D._____

_____

E._____

_____

F._____

_____

G._____

_____

H._____

_____

I._____

_____

J._____

_____

K._____

L._____

_____

M._____

_____

N._____

_____

O._____

_____

Other Books By Dr. Sesley Include:

FIRSTFRUITS: God's Plan to Propel You from Poverty to Prosperity

God's River of Prosperity (Swimming in the 100-Fold Flow and Beyond)

Daybreak: Lighting the Pathway of Following Jesus

So You Think You're Ready For Marriage?

To Order More Copies of this or other books by Dr. Sesley
Please Call the Toll Free, 24 hour, 7 day a week Order No.:
Go to our website: calvaryfi.com/bookstore or to amazaon.com

For Information on Booking Dr. Sesley to Speak at your church, seminar, conference or
event,

Contact Us at:

Visit us on the web at:

www.calvaryfi.com

Or email us at: contactus@calvaryfi.com

Or Call us @ (310) 766-6190

To Receive Coaching on Book Publishing, Leadership or Outreach

Visit Dr. Sesley's coaching website at

www.radicalcoaching.com

Check Out our Facebook Page at https://www.facebook.com/calvaryfellowshipinternational

Follow us on Twitter: www.twitter.com/pastorksesley

Please include your prayer requests and comments when you write. Thank You!

About the Author
ห้ห้

Kenneth Sesley is the Founding Senior Pastor Calvary Fellowship International, located in Carson, California. In 1980 God spoke to Kenneth and said: "Teach My people that they don't have to be Poor, Sick, or Ignorant (of things of the Spirit). Since then Pastor Sesley has taken the message of Faith, Prosperity, Divine Healing and the Gifts of the Spirit to the nation by ministering in local churches, conferences and conventions. The impact of Dr. Sesley's teaching and breakthrough anointing is attested to wherever he has gone.

In addition to pastoring a local church, whose vision is to be "a local church family of thousands of born-again, Bible believing, Spirit-filled followers of Jesus Christ by *Reaching, serving & loving humanity*, *Raising up fully equipped servants & leaders*, and *Reproducing an abundance of other healthy, culturally relevant, church planting churches* for the expansion of God's Kingdom in Carson, the South Bay, Southern California, across America and around the world", Dr. Sesley is also available to share the messages of faith, prosperity, healing, leadership, outreach, church growth, and healthy church systems across America and around the world in order to be a blessing to God's people and to fulfill God's assignment upon his life. Pastor Sesley has also established the Radical Coaching Network to raise up the next generation of leaders, pastors and authors.

If you are interested in becoming an author yourself and having your own book published, go to www.radicalcoaching.com for further information.

www.ingramcontent.com/pod-product-compliance
Lightning Source LLC
Chambersburg PA
CBHW081332090426
42737CB00017B/3100